INTERIM JUDAISM

T0337586

INTERIM JUDAISM

Jewish Thought in a Century of Crisis

Michael L. Morgan

Indiana University Press

Bloomington and Indianapolis

This book is a publication of
Indiana University Press
601 North Morton Street
Bloomington, IN 47404-3797 USA

http://iupress.indiana.edu

Telephone orders   800-842-6796
Fax orders   812-855-7931
Orders by e-mail   iuporder@indiana.edu

This book is based on the Samuel Goldenson Lectures delivered at the Hebrew
Union College–Jewish Institute of Religion, Cincinnati in 1999.

The paper used in this publication meets the minimum requirements of American
National Standard for Information Sciences—Permanence of Paper for Printed
Library Materials, ANSI Z39.48-1984.

Manufactured in the United States of America

Library of Congress Cataloging-in-Publication Data

Morgan, Michael L., date
    Interim Judaism : Jewish thought in a century of crisis / Michael L. Morgan.
       p.   cm.
    Includes bibliographical references and index.
    ISBN 0-253-33856-5 (cl : alk. paper) — ISBN 0-253-21441-6 (pa : alk. paper)
    1. Judaism—20th century. 2. Judaism—United States. 3. Revelation (Jewish
theology) 4. Redemption—Judaism. 5. Holocaust, Jewish (1939–1945)—
Influence.   I. Title.

BM565 .M63 2001
296.3'09'04—dc21
                                                                00-063465

1 2 3 4 5   06 05 04 03 02 01

To Shelly Zimmerman
Friend, Rabbi, Leader

CONTENTS

ACKNOWLEDGMENT

I WOULD LIKE to thank Shelly Zimmerman, the President of the Hebrew Union College–Jewish Institute of Religion, and the faculty of the College–Institute for the invitation to deliver the Goldenson Lectures. During my visits to Cincinnati from Bloomington, Dean Ken Ehrlich was a gracious and attentive host. Over the past several years, David Finkelstein has been a wonderful conversation partner; as we have talked about his work and mine, I have learned a great deal and regularly been provoked to think more precisely, carefully, and thoroughly about a number of issues raised in this book. David has been a great colleague and friend. Paul Franks and I have been working on Franz Rosenzweig for a couple of years, and that collaboration has meant a lot to me. I have also regularly enjoyed discussions with a number of other friends, especially Hindy Najman, John Efron, Jim Naremore, Peter Knobel, Steve Weitzman, and Mira Wasserman. Years ago, David Myers invited me to give a paper that was my first opportunity to write and talk about early-twentieth-century European, modernist thought. On Jewish matters, nothing I write would be possible if it were not for Emil Fackenheim, whose friendship is one of my life's greatest treasures. As always, when I finish a book, I think of Aud, Deb, and Sara, who make it all worthwhile.

INTRODUCTION

THIS BOOK GREW out of three Samuel Goldenson Lectures, delivered at the Hebrew Union College–Jewish Institute of Religion in Cincinnati in April, 1999. In the lectures and now in the book, I try to ask where Jewish life and Jewish thought in America find themselves at the turn of the twenty-first century. This question requires recovering the lessons of Jewish thought in the twentieth century as it sought to respond to the emergence of great urban, industrial cultures in Europe at the turn of the century, the catastrophic war and its aftermath, the Holocaust, the Cold War, the establishment of the State of Israel and its embattled situation, and the conflicts in postwar American society. These chapters do not aim at a comprehensive examination of these responses; rather, they are a preliminary probing of the territory, performed with the hope of bringing attention to some highlights and sketching a trajectory for future work.

Answering this question requires that I return to the most important thinking of the early part of the century, to what we might call modernist thought, as it was manifest in the lives and works of European intellectuals before and after World War I. This intellectual world, the world of Georg Simmel, Martin Buber, Georg Lukács, and Franz Kafka, of Gershom Scholem, Karl Barth, Siegfried Kracauer, and Walter Benjamin, of T. S. Eliot and Franz Rosenzweig, was extraordinarily creative and rich. It included novel and powerful understandings of many ideas important to what we might call the "religious sensibility." Poets, social thinkers, novelists, artists, philosophers, and theologians explored notions such as redemption and revelation; they confronted new human possibilities wrought by urbanization, modern technologies and discoveries, as well as the social and psychological developments we associate with modern cities and their culture; and they sought to shape some understanding of what human life might and, indeed, should be. Many of these intellectuals were Romantics or neo-Romantics; they eulogized artistic experience, mysticism, and the exotic. Many sought to break with the past or to return to it selectively. They aspired to new forms of redemption, new types of community, and distinctive types of human experience, all in the service of hope and aspiration. Some revered science, novelty, and new technologies; others abhorred them. To some, the outbreak of war in 1914 was an extraordinary opportunity for profound experience and heroism or the sign of the emergence of a new world; to others, it represented the horrors and evils of modern urban culture and all that accompanied it.[1]

In this book, I focus on three strands of the intellectual fabric of that period. All three were important then, remained important throughout the twentieth century, and continue to be important today. I explore what those three strands involved, how they developed in that early period, and how they might be appropriated today. The three strands deal with the problem of objectivity, the experience of the transcendent as a ground of objectivity, and the relationship between redemption and politics. In modernist culture, all three are frequently articulated in religious terms—such as redemption, revelation, messianism, eternity, and secular time or history. In each chapter, I discuss one of the strands as it developed in this period, among Jewish intellectuals and others, some of whom were assimilated or alienated Jews, non-Jews, or wholly secular figures. I then turn to the way in which that strand has manifested itself in American culture and intellectual life in the postwar period, after the Holocaust, and as the Holocaust became a part of American and Jewish self-awareness. How notions such as redemption and revelation can be recovered for Jewish life today depends not only upon the creativity of modernist attempts to wrestle with these themes, but also upon how, for us, the Holocaust and North American intellectual culture have shaped our situation. I conclude each chapter by suggesting how, in our situation, we can recover the strand in question and hence the resources we have for weaving the fabric of contemporary Jewish life and Jewish thought in America.

The ideas that I am dealing with here are abstract and general.

They have been in circulation for quite a long time; they permeate Jewish religious thought and in one form or another much of Western culture. Why do I begin with the modernist phase of their development? Why not return to the Enlightenment? Or to the seventeenth century? Or the medieval period? Or antiquity? To rabbinic Judaism and rabbinic texts or to the Bible? All of this history is important. Even very broad and abstract notions such as redemption can and should be recovered within a process of rethinking, clarifying, and debating the ways in which they were used and understood throughout Jewish intellectual life, from the Biblical period to our own. But I am convinced that with the rise of the new urban culture at the turn of the century in Berlin, Vienna, Paris, Prague, Budapest, and London, some very important changes took place, both in how people lived and experienced their lives and in their modes of thinking. I would contend that for an understanding of the ideas I deal with here—redemption and revelation, eternity and history, messianism and politics—the developments of this modernist period are so creative, so influential, and so integral to our self-understanding, that the most appropriate way to start to recover them is to begin here and to work both forward, to our time and, eventually, backward to earlier periods, earlier texts, and earlier worlds. So, I conceive of this book as the beginning of a larger project, launched from the place where the most creative and compelling thinking occurred.

To describe the three strands in a bit more detail, the first concerns the desire for objective standards for belief and practice and hence involves issues such as relativism and the rise of historicism. I call this the "problem of objectivity" and try to show how it emerged for many modernist thinkers in the early twentieth century, reemerged in postwar American culture, was deepened by the Holocaust and its impact on Jewish theology, and confronts us today. The second strand concerns the way we conceive of the human experience of the transcendent or divine. This is the traditional notion of revelation, an idea that underwent extremely imaginative discussion in the modernist period, especially regarding the question of mediation and language. Here I set out the debate between those who favored a conception of revelation as unmediated and direct and those who conceived it as mediated by language. I then ask how we, at the beginning of the twenty-first century with its intellectual and historical developments, might act in terms of this aspiration to some kind of access to the divine. Finally, the third strand involves redemption and its relationships with everyday, historical life. I call this the "problem of messianism and politics." In a variety of ways, I argue, this problem was utterly central to discussion in the modernist period, and it gave rise to some extremely interesting attempts to understand history and politics, on the one hand, and our communal and social goals, with redemption conceived as an ideal human community, on the other. Here too our appropriation of some model for religious life, that is lived in the world and yet equipped with some ultimate hopes and aspirations, is mediated by the Holocaust and by the thinking that responds to it.

In a sense, the three strands I trace cooperate to form a common emerging pattern in the fabric of Jewish life. That pattern has several distinctive characteristics. It may be described as a Jewish life that is active and practical without yet having achieved, if it ever will, theoretical clarity and comprehensiveness. It is also variegated and diverse, rather than uniform and consistent. Finally, it is interim and provisional, without a firm confidence that anything more secure is in the offing. Even in the modernist period, given the diverse and powerful influences on religious thinking, there was a strand that was realist and hesitant. Given the impact of the Holocaust and other historical and intellectual events, our own situation calls for a similar kind of searching and waiting, a Jewish life of experimentation and openness, of active involvement grounded in temporary convictions and not on theoretically secure views. We are at a moment of great uncertainty, lacking definitive answers; nonetheless, we recognize the mandate to a committed Jewish life. We must respond to it—seeking redemption with a small *r* and engaging in all that we can do to make ourselves receptive to the transcendent, even without the confidence that what we do will be fulfilled or even that fulfillment is in and of itself fully warranted. Much is based on hope, aspiration, waiting, and working, but none of these comes with complete certitude. The theological self-understanding that I arrive at is provisional and open-ended, appropriate, it would seem, for the turn of the twenty-first century. This book encourages a life of searching both for past and for future, a searching that dares to aspire and is yet cautious and modest.

INTERIM JUDAISM

1

THE PROBLEM OF OBJECTIVITY
BEFORE AND AFTER AUSCHWITZ

The Crisis of Objectivity

The twentieth century has been called a short century, beginning
with World War I in 1914 and ending with the fall of the Soviet
empire in 1989.[1] But the length and character of a century are not
always marked by such transforming events. One might just as use-
fully view the twentieth century as longer than one hundred years,
beginning with the emergence of nationalism in the late decades of
the nineteenth century, or at least with the dramatic urbanization
and industrialization of those decades, and continuing to the ad-
vanced information and communications, computer-based technologies of our own day. This latter view places its emphasis on the
revolutionary growth in technology and the transformation of life
in the cities of Europe that paved the way for the world in which
we now live. Whatever its length, the twentieth century was a period
of almost permanent disorientation. Population explosion, urban
growth, and new technologies left little of the world untouched and
few periods without widespread psychological dislocation.

At the beginning of the twentieth century, sociology and social
theory emerged out of the orbit of philosophy and took shape in
part as the study of life in the modern European city, a life charac-
terized by alienation, isolation, and despair. It is no small wonder
that when war exploded in August of 1914, vast numbers of intellectuals and artists found the conflagration exhilarating and elevat-
ing, an opportunity to revitalize lives that had been deadened by

regimentation and loneliness. Many others of course disagreed; to them the war was horrifying and virtually apocalyptic, the nemesis of all that modernity had come to mean.

This well-known dichotomy is as understandable as it is sad and even shocking. For this century of disorientation was also a century of reorientation and of the search for new orientation. Indeed, the challenges of the century—political, economic, technological, psychological, and cultural—were so dramatic and served so decisively to cut us off from the past that the need for reorientation was and continues to be virtually constant, if not for all, then certainly for most of us in the West. Literature and art, from expressionism and surrealism to pop art and minimalist poetry, have expressed the despair and the yearning that mark modern life—early in the century, after the Holocaust, and today. Often hope has been at best a sign of resignation and possibly an expression of false optimism or blindness. As a constant refrain, we hear a yearning to recover, to find solid ground, to find our way when we seem so lost.

This recurring and powerful dialectic marked life in the twentieth century. It is a dialectic of sickness and recovery, of crisis and resolution, of loss and redemption. In America, from the postwar years to the present, we have largely avoided using religious terms for this pattern, but in the early decades of the twentieth century, in Europe—in Berlin, Vienna, Paris, Prague, and Budapest—the terminology used by virtually all intellectuals—poets, novelists, artists, philosophers, social critics, and theologians—was religious. In his great unfinished novel, *The Man Without Qualities,* Robert Musil has one of his characters, General Stumm, refer to this terminology in the following terms:

> The intellectual types . . . were chronically dissatisfied . . . whichever way they turned, they found something wrong. . . . So they ended up convinced that their era was fated to be a spiritual wasteland that could be redeemed only by some special event or some very special personage. It was among the so-called intellectuals that the word "redemption" and its kin came into vogue at this time. They did not see how things could go on unless a messiah came quickly. . . . The

age before the Great War was a messianic age. . . . [There is a] conviction that without a spiritual dimension there can be no human life worthy of the name, but with too much of it there can be none either.[2]

One finds this "language of redemption" as readily in the work of Georg Lukács and Max Weber as one does in that of Karl Barth and Franz Rosenzweig. Musil himself saw the need for such redemptive action and associated it, in his essays and in his famous novel, with the achievement of a spiritual condition, akin to art, love, and mysticism, which he came to call "the other condition" (*der andere Zustand*). At virtually the same historical moment, T. S. Eliot completed *The Wasteland* and Rainer Maria Rilke his "Duino Elegies" in both of which we find a similar aspiration to unity, wholeness, and transcendence in a world destitute and deracinated.

Redemption of this kind is a matter of orientation, the goal of a life that has some directedness. Such orientation, by its very nature, must be objective.[3] If it were not, then that which gives our lives direction and meaning would change and thus the direction would change, thereby condemning it to instability; or the ground of orientation would depend upon varying or diverse conditions, which would make it insecure and unreliable; or the ground of orientation would be different for different individuals or groups and thus would involve competing claims to direction. Orientation of this deep and fundamental kind, then, must be objective, and thus must be permanent and absolute. The twentieth century was a century in search of such objectivity, of an unconditional, universal, and timeless ground for what gives our lives meaning and purpose.

The twentieth century promoted this search. But it also, time and again, registered serious intellectual doubts about the possibility of its success. At the century's beginning, figures such as Wilhelm Dilthey distinguished the human sciences from the natural sciences and identified the points of view characteristic of the two. One outcome of his project was an understanding of human experience as perspectival, historically embedded, and interpretive, and hence of the human world as shaped and organized differently by different groups, cultures, and periods. This discussion gave rise to a wide-spread commitment to relativism and historicism that took values and principles to be grounded in cultural differences and historical conditions. With this commitment came the risk of skepticism or nihilism and, for many, the concomitant yearning for a secure foundation for meaning and purpose.[4] From these beginnings and then throughout the twentieth century, the fragility of worldviews and values permeated continental thought, in Germany at first and then in France, albeit with episodes of counter-attack and response. In America, at least since the late seventies, these tendencies have emerged in the movements we now call collectively "postmodernism" and "multiculturalism." They are descendants of the earlier hermeneutical developments and the postwar existentialism that infused the undercurrent of despair in the fifties, percolated below the surface of the "culture of affluence," and then exploded in postwar literature, the beat movement, and the revolutionary sixties.

Throughout the twentieth century, there existed this "crisis of objectivity," a recurrent need to seek objective grounds for meaning and orientation and at the same time powerful reasons for doubting that the search could ever be fulfilled. It was not a parochial worry but rather a widespread crisis. Not surprisingly, it was also a crisis at the core of Jewish life in the twentieth century. Indeed, this crisis of objectivity has touched the Jewish people and Jewish life in especially profound and significant ways, both early in the century because of the Jewish role in modernity, the dynamics of Emancipation and dislocation, and modernist intellectual life in Europe and then late in the century because of the role of the Holocaust for Jewish life and Jewish thought. By looking more closely at some of its stages in European and American Jewish intellectual life, we stand to clarify something especially important about the crisis itself and about Jewish life, in the shadow of catastrophe.

The Problematic of Modernist European Culture

From 1899 to 1901, during his years of university study, Martin Buber spent time in Berlin and attended the lectures of Georg Simmel. Like so many others of the period, Buber was deeply influenced by Simmel, especially by his understanding of the alienated character of urban culture and the psychological plight of the individual. At the very time that Buber studied with him, Simmel was completing his monumental analysis of urban economy, society, and its psychological implications, *The Philosophy of Money,* published in 1900.[5] In it and in many essays and papers written from then until his death in 1918, Simmel described what he called a "tragedy of culture." This tragic situation was one of debilitating alienation between individuals and their labor, their neighbors, their cultural creations, and ultimately themselves.[6] By the decade of the war, Simmel had adopted the language of the popular *Lebensphilosophie* (Life Philosophy) associated with Nietzsche, Bergson, and others; he saw the tragedy as a permanent condition of the yearning of life to fulfill itself and the ways in which its forms tended to become ossified and crippling. In his words, the crisis and tragedy of culture was manifest in the tension between life and form, between the dynamic forces of life that require creative realization in cultural forms and yet that always aspire to constant creative freedom and vitality beyond these rigidified forms. As Georg Lukács put it in 1909, in an essay on Kierkegaard deeply indebted to Simmel's analysis and terminology, the problem of life is the problem of soul giving form to life. But form is static and fixed, while life is vital and always in flux. The crisis lies in the futility of life's needs and its limitations, of living what cannot be lived, of building a crystal palace out of air.[7]

Simmel was born of Jewish stock but brought up a Christian. He trained as a philosopher and wrote his dissertation on Kant. But his interests turned to social phenomena and the analysis of them, in particular those phenomena that distinguished life in the modern urban world. Simultaneously he developed a terminology and method for dealing with modern social roles and a critical analysis of the complexity and impact of modern urban life on human experience. Focusing his attention on detailed, probing analyses of particular types or roles, such as the prostitute, the poor, the stranger, and the adventurer, Simmel used these snapshots to expose the particular nature of life in the modern, industrial, bureaucratized urban setting. These are the so-called fragments of modernity that exemplify the psychological effects of modern urban life on the individual. Of special interest to Simmel, who spent most of his career lecturing in Berlin, were the psychological dimensions of culture—on the one hand the ways in which human beings created and shaped the cultural commodities, roles, and institutions in which they lived and then, on the other hand, how they then experienced the culture in which they participated. Simmel was interested in objective culture, artifacts and institutions, only insofar as he saw it as the fulcrum for the activities of subjective culture and especially as he saw it as the vehicle by which the self became alienated from its labor, its products, its roles, others, and ultimately itself.

Simmel's work reached an important plateau in the years from 1898 to 1912. During that period, he published several vital works: his monumental study of the economics and social psychology of the modern city, *The Philosophy of Money;* the important article based on the book, "The City and the Life of the Spirit"; and the essays that comprised his work on the "conflict of modern culture." At the same time, his fascination with art reached its apex, as did his conviction that art alone was capable of dealing with that conflict and resolving the crisis of culture as he conceived it.

Drawing on the earlier work of Marx and others, Simmel, in his epoch-making study of the modern urban world, concluded that the primary phenomenon that led to the ramified alienation of the self and the conflict between objective and subjective culture was the division of labor. It was this procedure, so determinative a feature of industrial life and productivity, that alienated the self from its products and from the very process whereby those products came into being. It was this process, too, that led to similar alienations on the part of the consumer. Simmel puts it this way in *The Philosophy of Money* (1900):

> Alienation results from "the growing division of labor," which, "understood in its widest sense to include the division of production, the differentiation of work processes and specialization, separates the working person from the work produced and endows the product with objective independence." (*The Philosophy of Money,* 63, 457)

This sentiment is repeated in the famous article of 1903, "The City and the Life of the Spirit." It goes back to Marx and points ahead to Lukács's famous account of reification in *History and Class Consciousness* (1923). In a world shaped by such division of labor and all it entails, the wholeness of the individual, manifest in primitive cultures and in the activities of genuine artists, is stunted. Unity between the creator and the created object is shattered, and the results are ramified into a multifaceted set of separations between the self and its actions, the self and the consumer, the self and natural resources, and ultimately the self and itself. As Simmel puts it, the division of labor leads to a conflict between subjective experience and objective culture, between life and form. In their ideal state, the two are unified, for the one expresses itself genuinely in the other. This occurs in primitive societies and in the work of genuine artists and perhaps best of all in primitive craftsmen and artisans. Hence, insofar as the modern self longs for wholeness and a recovery of this unity, insofar as it seeks to overcome this disintegration and fragmentation, it seeks modes of experience and activity that will do so, and it finds them above all in art. Early on, then, Simmel came to see the conflict between subjective experience and objective culture as a feature of all culture, not just modern culture, and he saw as well that art could, in principle, overcome that conflict and solve the problems it generated. It was through art that form could be brought to content in a unifying way. The Kantian roots of Simmel's optimism are evident.

But Simmel's confidence was short-lived. By 1911, when he wrote "The Conflict of Modern Culture," he had become convinced that the conflict or crisis was a permanent condition of all culture and that the problem it presented was insoluble. To be sure, he recalls how a solution would look:

> The ideal culture occurs "whenever life produces certain forms in which it expresses and realizes itself. . . . These forms encompass the flow of life and provide it with content and form, latitude and order." ("The Conflict of Modern Culture," 11)

But he no longer thinks that any experience or any activity, art included, can achieve that ideal:

Perhaps "life wishes here to obtain something which it cannot reach.
It desires to transcend all forms and to appear in its naked immediacy.
. . . Although this chronic conflict between form and life has become
acute in many historical epochs, none but ours has revealed it so
clearly as its basic theme." ("The Conflict of Modern Culture," 25)

At best, art may be a momentary and episodic anticipation of a
wholeness or unity that we all seek, but it cannot achieve that goal,
which forever remains beyond us. Culture, in short, is not a field of
challenge; it is instead a domain of tragedy.

For Simmel, the solution to the crisis of objectivity, orientation,
and redemption from this alienation, if at all possible, rested in the
life of the artist or the mystic, in separation from the pedestrian,
stultifying forms of bourgeois culture, and in the aspiration to a
unity beyond all diversity and fragmentation. But such lives suffered
the tension between their special calling and the attractions of
everyday life. This tension is powerfully expressed in the early life
and work of Simmel's student Georg Lukács. Lukács saw his own
plight reflected in Kierkegaard's momentous choice to sacrifice his
love for Regina Olsen in behalf of "the icy temple of nothing-but-
the-love-of-God."[8] Kierkegaard's decision was a leap of faith, nonetheless burdened by the temptations of marriage and domestic fulfillment.

"The tragedy of culture"—this was in fact the theme alluded to
in the title of the most famous of Georg Lukács's early essays, "The
Metaphysics of Tragedy."[9] It was a theme he had learned and appropriated from Simmel. Lukács was born of Jewish parents, but Judaism, he later recalls, played no role for his family or for him, and
eventually his family converted to Christianity. In Budapest, at the
turn of the century, his banker father was prominent and influential,
and he arranged for his precocious son to write drama reviews for a
local magazine. As a teenager Lukács became active in a progressive
drama company, the Thalia society, and cultivated an interest in literature, drama, and society. In 1906 he moved to Berlin to study
with Simmel, and there, at the encouragement of friends, he wrote
a work on the sociology of modern drama, influenced by Simmel,
which won a prestigious Hungarian award. He returned to Budapest

in 1909 and combined several of his essays into a volume called *Soul and Form*, published in Hungarian and then, a year later, in German, with two additional essays, the most important and most famous, "The Metaphysics of Tragedy," an essay on his friend, the playwright Paul Ernst. The central concepts of these essays—soul, form, life— are taken from Simmel and the *Lebensphilosophie* of the day. Like Simmel, Lukács had early been committed to the efficacy of art in bringing wholeness to fragmented modern life, in bringing "soul and form" to "life." But by the time he wrote these essays, his own experience had belied his optimism. He had come to see art and everyday life as irreconcilable; the choice between them was unconditionally exclusive.[10]

The tragedy was manifest to Lukács in the tension between his commitment to art, to drama and literature, and his love for another. The second, German edition of *Soul and Form* is dedicated to Irma Seidler, a young painter with whom Lukács had had a brief, intense relationship. At a crucial moment, however, he had decided to pursue his art and felt compelled to cut off the relationship. In November 1912, shortly before the essays were to be published in German, Seidler committed suicide, and Lukács dedicated them to her memory. They were, in short, his testimony to the irreconcilability of art with love for another—a powerful Romantic theme that arose again and again in these years to become a regular feature of the artistic temperament.

This theme—of the impossibility of art to bring form and soul to life, of the impossibility of being both an artist and a lover—is expressed beautifully in Lukács's essay on Kierkegaard, one of the earliest acts of recovery of that thinker for early-twentieth-century European thought. Lukács's own tragedy with Irma Seidler is Kierkegaard's, without the latter's optimism that his leaving Regina Olsen was not a permanent loss. Kierkegaard had believed that by sacrificing Regina Olsen and devoting himself wholly to God, he would ultimately obtain both. What Kierkegaard had sought to perform was what Lukács called a "gesture," an act of bringing form to life, of uniting transcendence and immanence, the absolute with the conditioned. But, Lukács judges, Kierkegaard did not see the futility in the gesture; he thought it could succeed, but he was wrong.

> The value of gesture! In other words: the value of form in life, the life-creating, life-enhancing value of forms. . . . form is perhaps the absolute's only road to life. . . . The gesture alone expresses life—but is it possible to express life? Is not this the tragedy of every art of life, that it wants to build a crystal palace out of air, to forge realities from the insubstantial possibilities of the soul. . . . Kierkegaard wagered his whole life on a gesture. . . . but can there really be a gesture vis-à-vis life? . . . Kierkegaard's heroism was that he wanted to create forms from life. His honesty was that he saw the crossroads and journeyed to the end of the road he had chosen. His tragedy was that he wanted to live what cannot be lived. (*Soul and Form*, 28 and 40)

Here is Simmel's final judgment reaffirmed: the tragedy of modern culture is a lost unity that we seek but that we cannot achieve; it is the effort to live what cannot be lived. Here, as Lukács puts it, is the task that art, like Kierkegaard's religious leap of faith, seeks to accomplish, "to build a crystal palace out of air." Unity and wholeness are the goal of all art, to overcome the fragmentation of the self that exiled the soul from others, nature, and indeed from all authenticity and meaning. The tragedy of life is to want and to aspire to what cannot be achieved in this world. But if the tragedy is that this form of redemption cannot be achieved, the security for the individual is that this is indeed the task or direction of the soul. Art and creativity express life in the deepest sense, and they give the soul a genuine, secure, objective, if unattainable, goal.

Lukács was devastated by Irma Seidler's suicide. For some months, guilt plagued him; he had abandoned her and left her without love and without support, and the result was her death. But, finally, Lukács was able to transcend his grief and to see his way clear to the possibility of some kind of redemption. In a powerful dialogue, "On Poverty of Spirit," published in the short-lived journal—*A Szellem* (The Spirit)—which Lukács co-edited, he comes to accept the possibility of a redemption not humanly realized but rather bequeathed as an act of grace by a Goodness that is transcendent. What art can achieve is not this messianic moment but rather the preparation for it, that emptying of the soul of all hindrances and encumbrances which the mystics conceived as impoverishing the spirit. Lukács's infatuation with mysticism and its association with artistic creativity, at least then in 1912, was not with their capacity to reach beyond the everyday world. It was, rather, with the mystic's joint realization that human life does have an authentic redemptive goal and yet that no redemptive moment could occur until the soul is unburdened by the affairs of this world. For Lukács in 1912, what art and mysticism could see was the objectivity of the meaning and purpose of human life; what human effort could not accomplish on its own was the realization of this redemptive goal.

The tension in the creative artist between everyday life and the demands of art is a romantic theme that was virtually ubiquitous among artists in our period, from Rodin and Rilke to Kafka and Agnon. What was also shared was the conviction or at least the hope that a life without secure direction, meaning, or purpose could be somehow linked to an objective ground for such direction. Martin Buber certainly felt this way, in his early years, during the period prior to World War I. He was enthralled with literature and poetry, with mystical experience, with the aspiration to a transcendent unity, and with the links between this conglomerate and Judaism. Once he completed his dissertation on the mystics Nicholas of Cusa and Jakob Boehme in 1904, he immersed himself in Hasidic texts and in a wide variety of mystical testimonies; his retellings of the legends of the Baal Shem Tov and of the tales of Nachman of Bratslav made him famous, and they were accompanied, almost simultaneously, with anthologies of mystical testimonies and Chinese legends and tales. By 1908, when he was invited to Prague by the young Zionists of the Bar Kochba Society, Buber was already a celebrity, an heroic exemplar of an effort to excavate deep, neo-Romantic veins in Judaism as an alternative to bourgeois Jewish formality. But his persona as an emblem of Jewish renewal was not parochial. At just about the same time, Buber corresponded with Lukács about Kierkegaard and Hasidism, commenting favorably on Lukács's essay on Kierkegaard and receiving with good grace Lukács's praise for Buber's Hasidic books, praise reiterated in a review of the books which Lukács published in Hungarian in 1911. When he traveled to Prague, then, in 1908, when he met with Robert Welsch, Hugo Bergmann, Max Brod, Hans Kohn, and the other young Bar Kochbans and gave the first of his three speeches, Buber was deeply immersed in a very wide-reaching project, to respond to the spiritual crisis of modern urban culture by locating and linking oneself to an objective ground of meaning and direction.

In Buber's writings of these years, as in the essays of Lukács and those of Simmel, redemption takes the shape of unity, an ultimate unity of divine or transcendent status. If there is going to be a solution to worldly alienation and its implications, that solution will have to begin with a transcendent ground and involve some human means of becoming linked to it. Art and mystical experience are seen as the dominant means.

One of the high points of this period in Buber's career, in which mysticism played such a central role, was the publication, in 1909, of a set of mystical writings from throughout the world, entitled *Ecstatic Confessions*. To his selection of these testimonies, Buber appended an important essay, "Ecstasy and Confession," which deals with the problem of language and its relation to the mystical experience itself and hence with the very possibility of mystical testimonies. In this essay he makes crystal clear that mysticism itself is an attempt to confront the bewildering commotion of everyday experience and to seek to transcend it through the self's merging with unconditional unity. In this way the mystic gains access to a wholly transcendent unity and, through unconditional detachment from the world, achieves or attains that unity. Hence, mystical experience essentially involves a dissolution of self and a transcendence of all the multiplicity that constitutes everyday experience and everyday language. How, then, Buber asks, can there be mystical confessions that testify to this ineffable experience in which self and other, subject and object dissolve into unity itself? Buber's answer is that these confessions are themselves not representations of the content of the experience, nor are they expressions of its phenomenology. Rather they are responses in language in which the self is moved by the impact of the experience to communicate its power and its significance. Primary among the vehicles of such response is the association of the experience with God and the use of myth to do so.

> One cannot burden the general run of occurrences with this experience; one does not dare to lay it upon his own poor I . . . ; so one hangs it on God. And what one thinks, feels and dreams about God then enters into his ecstasies, pours itself out upon them in a shower of images and sounds, and creates around the experience of unity a multiform mystery. ("Ecstasy and Confession," 4)

As Buber understands it, mystical and ecstatic experience is itself an aspiration to transcend the commotion of everyday life and its varied estrangements and divisions. In itself it is both access to unconditional unity and the attainment of a unity beyond articulation and expression. At the same time, insofar as the mystic's experience is limited and momentary and because the mystic is nonetheless a flesh-and-blood person living in the world, ecstatic experience gives rise to response, in part to a pouring out of images and sounds, which "creates around the experience of unity a multiform mystery" associated invariably with what one calls God.

But if Buber's affinity for mystical experience ended here, there is little reason to see it as going beyond Simmel's resignation or Lukács's hope. Buber, however, does not stop here. It is important to recall that at the same time that Buber was immersed in the philosophical problem of individuation and the tradition of mystical experience and confessions, he was also associated with a socialist organization, founded by the brothers Julius and Heinrich Hart and called *"Die Neue Gemeinschaft"* (The New Community). Here, in 1898, he delivered an early talk on community,[11] and here he met Gustav Landauer, socialist and student of mysticism, who was to become one of his most influential friends and heroes.[12]

Moreover, during the early years of Zionist activity Buber was an avid participant in the development of a non-political, cultural Zionism that conceived of that movement and its youth cohorts as a vanguard in the seeking of a renewal of Judaism in the modern world. First and foremost, Zionism was, to Buber, a commitment to revitalizing the Jewish experience and Jewish life and to understanding the role of Judaism in the history and destiny of humankind. To be sure, Zionism involved political activity and a desire for a return to the Jewish homeland, but to Buber these goals were subordinate to its central task, to return Judaism to its ancient and still relevant task, to return the world of the spirit to the world of the everyday.

Buber, that is, had found the ground of objectivity in the absolutely transcendent, but that objectivity needed to give direction to human life, life in the world. Objectivity is no redemptive solution unless it installs an orientation to embodied, worldly human existence. Buber, after his decade of immersion in mystical texts and ideas, found a very precise way of joining his commitment to mystical groundedness to Jewish life. He had of course been an early advocate of Zionism in the first decade of Herzl's Zionist movement. But his differences with Herzl were deep, and after losing political battles in 1901 and 1902, Buber had largely set aside active Zionist participation as he pursued his doctorate and devoted himself to the study of mysticism. The call from Prague was an invitation for him to return boldly to Jewish life, this time as a leader of young Prague Jews seeking a new mode of Jewish existence.

His first lecture, delivered in 1908, was a call to Jewish renewal based on his appropriation of *Lebensphilosophie* and the primacy of decision and commitment. When he returned, in March 1910, he gave a second speech, this time on the role of Judaism in the life of humankind. Here, in a paradigmatic way, he defines the Jewish task as one of aspiring to unity and then seeking to realize it in the world, to teach humanity what unity is and how it should be brought to Jewish life. Objectivity and transcendence, in other terms, make a claim upon the Jewish people; this is God's claim, to understand the dualisms and fragmentation of the worldly situation and to show the way to realizing unity in history—through the idea of the one God, the advocacy of justice, the creation of genuine community, and the propagation of the messianic idea.[13] Here Buber shows how mystical experience is not a goal of Judaism. Rather, it is a vehicle by which the Jewish self is oriented to action in the world, action that seeks to bring unity to realization in the here and now. Not only does the fire of mystical experience register a "multiform mystery"; it also issues in real action in the world, redemptive action.

> It is this striving for unity that has made the Jew creative. . . . Striving to evolve unity out of the division of the human community, he conceived the idea of universal justice. . . . Striving to evolve unity out of the division of the world, he created the messianic ideal, which later, again under the guiding participation of Jews, was reduced in scope, made finite, and called socialism. ("Judaism and Mankind," from *Three Addresses*, 28)

The experience of an undifferentiated and pure unity is not a goal; it is a moment of revelation, as it were, that issues in testimony and action, the latter expressed in the aspiration to social justice and equal treatment for all. If Buber is right, then Simmel and the early Lukács are wrong. Unity is not episodic and ultimately transcendent; the crisis of modernity and culture is not permanent. Rather, the experience of unity, whether in art or in mysticism, yields redemptive results, which are results for the world and not beyond it.

Couched in the vocabulary of mysticism that he had come to cultivate, this conception of Jewish renewal remained with Buber in subsequent years, even after the development of his philosophy of dialogue, and it later became the core of his conception of the Biblical message.[14]

But even in these early years, prior to the development of his doctrine of I-Thou, Buber's thinking, like Franz Rosenzweig's in the same period, builds on the debates of Dilthey and others about the distinctive character of the human sciences. Buber does not question the reality of a transcendent ground insofar as it is the object of ecstatic experience; what he focuses on is the way in which access to it is achieved, how language and myth are related to the experience of what is ineffable, and then how Jewish renewal should be configured as a life of worldly action, the building of unity and community. All of this is indebted to a view of human experience and action as perspectival, personal, and imbedded in the world and in history.

Structurally, we find something similar in other theological developments of the period. The Christian theological movement associated with figures like Karl Barth, Friedrich Gogarten, Rudolf Bultmann, and Paul Tillich, largely a movement of the early Weimar years, can be understood along the same lines. Here too there is a discontent with bourgeois morality and religion, with its focus on the human rather than the divine, on history and human psychology, and hence on the risks of relativism and a loss of groundedness. And there is also a turn to a kind of theocentric or transcendent attitude, a focus on God as the locus of orientation and direction. Finally, there is a continuing effort to tie the identification of this transcendence as central and determinative to life in this world and to the human problems of historical existence. In Barth, especially, there is a persisting struggle, once his "radical theology" begins to take shape as he works on the first edition of his *Romerbrief* (Commentary on Paul's *Letter to the Romans*) in the years up to 1918–1919, to maintain a clear sense of what this new primacy of God and revelation means for his socialism. How does revelation conceived as an act of divine love demand a socialist response to economic and political problems?

As I have pointed out, all of these figures and many others—from Simmel, Weber, Lukács, and Bloch to Buber, Barth, and Rosenzweig, from social critics and historians, to theologians and artists—were responding both to reality and to ideas. They were part of a world unsettled by enormous population shifts, rapid urban development, new inventions, social and psychological changes, and finally war; at the same time, they were challenged by new ways of thinking about human life, history, experience, language, knowledge, and more. In a figure like T. S. Eliot, for example, both dimensions of the modernist world had telling effect.

Eliot's early career and poetry, from "The Love Song of J. Alfred Prufrock" in 1911 to *The Wasteland* in 1922–1923, began with a sensitivity for the desperate futility and alienation characteristically found in Paris, London, and all of modern urban society. It is a picture which he learned in Paris when, during the year after he had completed his undergraduate studies at Harvard in 1910, he first came under the influence of French symbolist poetry, especially the

poems of Jules Laforgue, and the thought of Henri Bergson.[15] After
his year in Paris, he traveled to Munich in 1911, prior to his return
to Harvard to study philosophy. It was in that year that Eliot's talent
began to measure up to the task of representing poetically the fragmentation of the self and the despair and indecisiveness of modern
existence. Written under the influence of Bergson and Dostoyevsky,
"The Love Song of J. Alfred Prufrock" made an emblem of this
desperate futility, mingling the significant and the trivial and shat-
tering the self and its unstable, flowing experiences.

> Let us go then, you and I,
> When the evening is spread out against the sky
> Like a patient etherised upon a table;
> Let us go, through certain half deserted streets,
> The muttering retreats
> Of restless nights in one-night cheap hotels
> And sawdust restaurants with oyster-shells:
> Streets that follow like a tedious argument
> Of insidious intent
> To lead you to an overwhelming question . . .
> Oh, do not ask, "What is it?"
> Let us go and make our visit.
> ("The Love Song of J. Alfred Prufrock," lines 1–12)

Divided into an everyday self and a literary persona, Eliot's narrator
is both you and I, an everyday self and a deeper self, both of whom
wander the streets, avoiding resolution and burdened with unasked
questions and the tedium of all that they experience. In Eliot's poetic psyche, modern urban existence takes its toll; what emerges is a
portrait of alienation and a deep hunger for wholeness.

Upon his return to Harvard, Eliot began three years of study
(1911–1914) with Josiah Royce and others, in pursuit of a doctorate
in philosophy. These years marked the second stage in his early
thinking. In Royce's seminar, Eliot delivered a paper on ritual in
primitive culture and learned from Royce, whose *The Problem of
Christianity* appeared in 1913, the perspectival nature of human experience and interpretation and the role of community in the interpretive construction of the religious world. Royce and others led

him to idealism and especially to the work of F. H. Bradley, whose philosophy was at the center of the British appropriation of Hegel and the tradition of German Idealism. Here, in idealist philosophy if anywhere, the fragmented self and the multiple perspectives of human experience are taken to be unified in the Absolute; the problems of disunity and alienation and meaninglessness and the need for a ground of objective wholeness could be solved. In 1914–1916 Eliot traveled to Oxford and London to work with the Oxford idealist Harold H. Joachim on a dissertation on Bradley—*Knowledge and Experience in the Philosophy of F. H. Bradley*—a work completed but never defended. Perhaps the central lesson that Eliot learned from the study of Bradley was that while the perspectives or the standpoints that we as individuals take are varied and multiple, there is a need for unity and wholeness. At this precise point, however, Eliot registered his doubts. Bradley saw clearly that all of us experience the world as "finite centres," as he called them, and that there is a need to unify them into an absolute unity. However, Bradley could only posit such a unity arbitrarily. Eliot's insight was that philosophy can expose the demand and the need; however, it could not achieve the result. That must be left for poetry.[16]

> Bradley's universe, actual only in finite centres, is only by an act of faith unified. Upon inspection, it falls away into the isolated finite experiences out of which it is put together. . . . The Absolute responds only to an imaginary demand of thought, and satisfies only an imaginary demand of feeling. Pretending to be something which makes finite centres cohere, it turns out to be merely the assertion that they do. (*Knowledge and Experience*, 202)

> For the life of a soul does not consist in the contemplation of one consistent world but in the painful task of unifying (to a greater or lesser extent) jarring and incompatible ones, and passing, when possible, from two or more discordant viewpoints to a higher which shall somehow include and transmute them. (*Knowledge and Reality*, 147–148)

In these two passages we find Eliot judging Bradley as deficient; the latter recognized the need to unite the "finite centres" of experience but could not achieve it. What the soul needs to accomplish is not to contemplate the world as a whole; it needs to carry out the task of unifying that world by uniting its own and all particular standpoints into an absolute, unified standpoint.[17]

What the soul must accomplish, then, is to unify "jarring and incompatible" experiences, moving from "two or more discordant experiences" to another which somehow unifies them. By 1919, when Eliot wrote his essay "The Metaphysical Poets," he had come to believe that this is the task of the poet.

> When a poet's mind is perfectly equipped for its work, it is constantly amalgamating disparate experience; the ordinary man's experience is chaotic, irregular, fragmentary. The latter falls in love, or reads Spinoza, and these two experiences have nothing to do with each other, or with the noise of the typewriter or the smell of cooking; in the mind of the poet these experiences are always forming new wholes. ("The Metaphysical Poets," 64, in *Selected Prose*)

No passage could be more explicit about the poetic task, and when we juxtapose it, as I have done, with the passages from Eliot's dissertation, we see exactly how Eliot had come to believe that the poetic experience itself "forms new wholes" out of discordant, chaotic, fragmentary experiences. Moreover, Eliot understood how similar this poetic act is to mystical experience; they are akin, both episodes of unification.

> . . . what can only be called mystical experience happens to many men who do not become mystics. . . . A piece of writing meditated, apparently without progress, for months or years, may suddenly take shape and word. . . . he to whom this happens assuredly has the sensation of being a vehicle rather than a maker. . . . You may call it communion with the Divine, or you may call it a temporary crystallization of the mind. ("The Pensees of Pascal," 237–238, in *Selected Prose*)

In this essay, written some years later and explicitly about Pascal's *Pensees*, Eliot noted how mystical experience can occur to the poet, as it does to the religious adept, and this same type of experience, which earlier he had called "amalgamating disparate experience," he here called a "temporary crystallization of mind" or "communion with the Divine." Robert Musil, in 1923 in an essay on the film criticism of Béla Balázs, would call this type of experience, generically, "the other condition" and like Eliot would include within it the artistic experience together with that of mystics and lovers. Eliot had concluded, then, that the Absolute cannot simply be asserted by philosophy, nor does it come to human experience through an act of grace. Rather it must be "earned," so to speak, and the agent of that achievement is the poet.[18]

Nowhere does Eliot better exemplify this type of poetic act, this "crystallization of mind" whereby disparate and chaotic experiences and fragments are unified into a "new whole," than in *The Wasteland*. Indeed, one might argue that to exemplify the poetic act conceived in this way was the primary goal of the epoch-making poem.[19] This is not the occasion for even a cursory reading of that difficult but momentous work. Fortunately we can point to one text, Eliot's own, where this point is made and made explicitly. It is Eliot's famous note on the blind seer Tiresias.

> Tiresias, although a mere spectator and not indeed a "character," is yet the most important personage in the poem, uniting all the rest. Just as the one-eyed merchant, seller of currants, melts into the Phoenician Sailor, and the latter is not wholly distinct from Ferdinand Prince of Naples, so all the women are one woman, and the two sexes meet in Tiresias. What Tiresias *sees*, in fact, is the substance of the poem. (Eliot's note to line 218 of *The Wasteland*, CPP, 52)

The substance of the poem, that is, the unity by which all the episodes, characters, and more cohere, is in what Tiresias, the blind seer, sees. The object of his seeing is the substance of the poem. It is also the point of the poem, that is, the unity in his seeing. Tiresias is the poet's deputy, his agent, his representative. His seeing brings unity to the whole, and that unity, the product of the poetic act, is the substance of the poem and indeed, for Eliot at this time, of poetry itself.

With Eliot, then, we see captured a central feature of understanding the plight of life in the modern world, that for each individual it involves myriad standpoints or "finite centres," a vast array of fragmented, mundane, everyday experiences and more elevated ones as well. Thinking must begin with the multiplicity of the experiencing self. Eliot learned this truth from Bergson and Royce, but he might also have learned it from Dilthey as Buber did or from any number of other philosophers of the period. Moreover, this fragmentation was at the core of the plight of modern life, and to overcome it was the goal of individual experience and ultimately of social and political action as well. First, however, an emblem or intimation of a worldly unity must be grasped by the individual, and this, for Eliot, was the synthesis provided through poetic or mystical experience. In his influential essay of 1919, "Tradition and the Individual Talent," he appreciated how each new poetic achievement reconfigures the entire poetic tradition and in this way the present reshapes the past as it is shaped by it.

> Tradition . . . cannot be inherited, and if you want it you must obtain it by great labour. It involves, in the first place, the historical sense . . . [which] involves a perception, not only of the pastness of the past, but of its presence; the historical sense compels a man to write not only with his own generation in his bones, but with a feeling that the whole of the literature of Europe from Homer and within it the whole of the literature of his own country has a simultaneous existence and composes a simultaneous order. . . . No poet, no artist of any art, has his complete meaning alone. . . . you must set him, for contrast and comparison, among the dead. . . . The necessity that he shall conform, that he shall cohere, is not onesided; what happens when a new work of art is created is something that happens simultaneously to all the works of art which preceded it. The existing monuments form an ideal order among themselves, which is modified by the introduction of the new (the really new) work of art among them. ("Tradition and the Individual Talent," 38–39, in *Selected Prose*)

Eliot situated the poet within the tradition of poetry and then noted how that tradition is newly shaped every time a new poem of significance is added to it. Hence, the powerful poet not only makes new wholes out of the multiple fragments of disparate experience; he or she also makes a new whole out of the poetic tradition each time he or she creates a new poem to be added to it.

Like Buber, Lukács, and Simmel, then, Eliot too saw the problem of objectivity and redemption, for him a problem of wholeness and unity, as wrought by modern life and culture and identified by philosophy. In his eyes, however, the problem is only to be solved by poetry, by a creative act of synthesis. This solution smacks of aestheticism, of course, and of a kind of anthropocentrism that one does not find in Buber or the early Lukács or Barth. Nonetheless, Eliot too is responding to the crisis we have been discussing.

Buber's development of his philosophy of dialogue, Barth's work on his theology of crisis, and Franz Rosenzweig's writing of *The Star of Redemption* all took place in the waning years of the war and in its immediate aftermath. They were all responses to the crisis of objectivity that I have been describing. Barth admitted explicitly that as he sat in Safenwil, during the early weeks of the war, it was the public manifesto in support of the war, prepared by his teacher Adolf von Harnack and signed by his most revered teachers, that went off like a bomb in his intellectual armory.[20] What led him to seek new foundations was the recognition that the old liberal theology of his teachers, especially those at Marburg, could endorse the war and not see that it was grounded in greed, competition, and hubris. The war played a role in Buber's shift from a devotion to mystical experience to a more thoroughgoing commitment to community and interpersonal relationships, and it also was involved in Rosenzweig's theological development and his views about history, politics, and religion. But in all three, the real foundation of their searching and their aspiration was what the war brought powerfully to their attention: the need to find an objective, transcendent, detached, and independent ground for direction and meaning in Jewish and Christian life.

Objectivity and Its Nemesis

As I have described it, the crisis of objectivity may seem to be a scene of potential heroism. I have sketched the situation in terms of a very commonplace narrative, with the crisis portrayed as a threat and those who confront it as noble warriors of meaning and purpose that is secure and firm, timeless and unchangeable. If one takes the crisis as including only the question of a ground of objectivity and as asking only whether our values, meaning, and purpose in life are objective or relative, stable or in flux, then the whole matter can be understood as value neutral. There is no reason to think that seeking objectivity is a good thing and finding it an achievement. On the other hand, if one thinks that for many the problem, politically and socially, leads to widespread skepticism about moral direction, about values that we care about and that we take to be ingredients of a wholesome and rich life, and that for others it leads to nihilism, then one might well see the crisis as a real, concrete threat to society, to culture generally, and to human life. Although I will not argue the point here, I think that many early-twentieth-century European intellectuals do take the crisis to be such a threat. Hence, objectivity is not only a solution to the problem in some formal or abstract sense; it is also an urgent and desirable solution, for it looks as if its formal features—universality, timelessness, stability, reliability, and so forth—will contribute to overcoming skepticism and nihilism and therefore to flourishing human life.

But this conviction may be shortsighted or mistaken. There is a powerful argument against the desirability of objectivity, as we have discussed it, and it is extremely attractive when seen in an historical light. I have been valorizing the quest for objectivity and especially its accomplishment, the argument goes, when in fact, historically, it is clear that its desirability is refuted by history itself. Scholars such as Fritz Stern, George Mosse, Eberhard Jaeckel, Uriel Tal, and Saul Friedlander have shown that Nazism itself arose as a solution to the problem of objectivity. It emerged out of neo-Romantic, Volkish, and conservative thinking that was aimed at solving the problems of relativism, historicism, and skepticism that accompanied the new culture of urban Europe, rapid industrialization, the breakdown of traditional society and norms, the war, and the development of new ideas about history and human experience. Absolutism of this kind—what Friedlander, after Tal, calls "redemptive antisemitism" —may look like a version of mere ethnocentrism and parochialism, but it is conceived as an unconditional, universal, eternal worldview. History shows that the very crisis we have been discussing in fact led to Nazi fascism and totalitarianism. Ought we not, on reflection, simply to reject objectivity altogether, rather than risk a recurrence of such a horrific outcome?[21]

It is unnecessary to debate the historical scholarship of those who have tried to show that Nazism was a development of certain clearly identifiable trends and directions in German culture and that socially, politically, and historically, the setting for its emergence involved social dislocation, the war, and economic crisis, as well as the intellectual challenges that we associate with relativism and historicism, Nietzschean among them. The work of the people I mentioned above is now widely accepted, and our understanding of the growth of Nazi totalitarianism has been enriched importantly by it. But what does this conclusion mean? Surely no one would want to say that the search for objectivity in science, morality, and religion necessarily leads to political absolutism and totalitarianism.

Siegfried Kracauer was an important critic of Weimar culture, contributor to and editor of the *feuilleton* page for the *Frankfurter Zeitung* from 1920–1933.[22] With the help of friends, Kracauer was able to flee Paris in 1940 for the United States. In the forties, he worked on a project for the Museum of Modern Art and the U.S. government on German film and the use of film for Nazi propaganda. His famous book, *From Caligari to Hitler,* on Nazi propaganda films and German expressionist cinema, was published in 1947. Part of Kracauer's social and psychological conclusion was that films like Leni Riefenstahl's *Triumph of the Will* (1935) grew directly out of German film in the Weimar years. Surely, however, we should not infer from this (and Kracauer did not) that German film in Weimar, all of it, in form, style, and so forth, is culpable and is to be rejected, opposed, and disposed of. There is no justification for such a reaction.

How, then, should one argue? It is that seeking objective, unconditioned grounds for our beliefs and actions, for our social programs and political models, runs the *risk* of leading to absolutism and totalitarianism. Developments prior to and following World War II are too recent, too vivid, too horrific. Therefore, if the search for objective grounds can lead to "redemptive antisemitism," then no search for objectivity and for a conception of redemption for social life is worth the risk. We are better off living with no absolutes, no objective grounds, no transcendence.

It is clear that once put in these terms, the argument against objectivity appeals to one's sense of threat and to one's judgment about relative advantage over risk. But, in fact, there is more to the argument. The skeptic is not simply asking us to be cautious; he or she is not simply urging us to take history seriously. The skeptic is asking us to do much more—in fact, to do what we are virtually unable to do.

There are those who would argue that relativism of a total or global kind is incoherent, either self-refuting or artificial and pointless. Let us put this kind of response aside. To the skeptic seeking objectivity, relativism—at least of an everyday and non-technical kind—is indeed a genuine option. There is an alternative to trying to find objective grounds for our beliefs and actions; it is to let people, societies, cultures, and other groups have their due—to let them believe what they will and claim what they will. To the skeptic, life without Meaning can still be life with meaning, but my meaning and yours differ. We can celebrate difference or at least accept it, tolerate it. The best way to respond to Nazi totalitarianism and its products is to oppose all totalitarianisms, all absolutes, and all claims to objectivity.

Unfortunately, however, the skeptic, I do not believe, actually wants to go far with this conviction, and if he or she does want this openness to be unconditional, without limits, then he or she wants us to sever a very significant connection that we have with the past, with Western culture, and with much that we value about it. Moreover, he or she wants us to live in ways we cannot live, to act and live without convictions of any kind.

Why? The aspiration to objectivity, to a firm and general understanding of the world, about our lives and about our conduct and attitudes, has been a pervasive feature of Western culture and not of it alone. It is reflected in the historical developments that we associate with religion, science, morality, politics, philosophy, psychology, and much else. Whether we take objectivity to be based on power and control, or rationality and understanding, or love and concern, each of these domains of human experience, such as religion and science, has within the course of Western history maneuvered between the poles of achieving greater stability, security, reliability, and timelessness, on the one hand, and greater variability, instability, changeability, and temporality, on the other. For many, all along the way, the prior values have been dominant. At crucial junctures, in trying to understand natural phenomena of all kinds, people have sought an understanding that could be counted on, that one could act on, believe in, commit to, and that would be stable or hold forever. In trying to design or redesign forms of governance, people have sought security, peace, and well-being, or they have suffered, thinking that such suffering too was stable and firm. In short, each in its own way—with religion, science, and morality, for example—has sought strategies for achieving objectivity. Looking back on the ways in which the seeking was done and what the results were, we are not always satisfied or pleased; objectivity does not guarantee a happy outcome nor a completely desirable one. But all along, whatever kind of solution was sought for local problems and issues, it was always part of a larger project, to find a stable, firm, and timeless order. To deny that project has been to deny something that seems fundamental to "human nature" or to a permanent aspiration of the human condition. We want and have always wanted to understand the world not just from our particular limited point of view but from "everyone's" point of view, to determine not just how I or you should act but how "everyone" should act, all the time, and to find a way to be related to some ultimate locus of responsibility, power, and justification not simply for me or you but for everyone. When an action occurs, we want to know why it was performed; we want to know the agent's reasons or what caused him or her to act. And the more general the reasons or the causes, the more understandable the act. Thomas Nagel calls this aspiration a desire to find "the view from nowhere."[23] It is older than Aristotle, than Plato, than Parmenides, even than Moses and Abraham. And it has not gone away. All of us acknowledge it daily and operate according to it. In our everyday lives, when we live together, talk, deliberate, make decisions, agree or disagree, cooperate or conflict, we want those things that we associate with objectivity. We do not argue with each other if all we want is to express our views, let you express yours, and leave it at that. We argue because each of us believes that he or she is right and each wants the other to accept what he or she believes, or at least to recognize that our belief is justified. Even the skeptic wants that, which is part of what makes the skeptic hard-put to "argue" with us about objectivity. We should be on our guard about the content of our views, if we are going to seek grounds for their objectivity and claim that they are objective, but we should not, because we cannot, give up the search for them or for their grounds. That would be to ask us to be something we are not.

The lesson of Nazi totalitarianism and the Holocaust—the extermination process that led to and included the killing squads, the death camps, and the gas chambers—lies elsewhere. It warns us, in a way that virtually nothing else could, about possibility; it warns us to be on our guard, so that as we, like our predecessors, try to meet for ourselves the crisis of objectivity, we do so with the proper moral and, for some, religious attentiveness. It warns us against the moral risks of both relativisms and absolutisms. What it does not teach us is to abandon that search completely.

Objectivity, Postwar Intellectual Culture, and Post-Holocaust Jewish Thought

The growth and development of Nazi fascism, the extermination of European Jewry, the death camps, the Holocaust (as I shall call them collectively)—these phenomena did not resolve this problematic; indeed, they deepened it and in deepening it, they have made it seem to us, as we stand on our side of the great divide, more difficult, more urgent, yet more paradoxical. After the Holocaust, objectivity is both more dubious and more necessary than it had seemed before. Why is this so?

On the one hand, the suffering and atrocity were so deep and so profound that all honest responses to the Holocaust must seek to stay with its utter historicity and refuse flight into the abstract, the detached, and the universal. Serious encounters with the Holocaust refuse to cordon off or quarantine the event in any way and to leave untouchable practices, theories, ideas, or principles that are immune to it. There simply is no such immune intellectual or practical precinct. None of our concepts or categories remain the same, and this means that in principle all our thinking is historicized, relativized, and qualified; there are no absolutes. On the other hand, there must be such immunity, for the evil and the horror were so great that only some kind of resistance, unconditional and irrevocable, is acceptable and honest. If there is one thing we know after the death camps, it is that all cruelty and certainly all genocidal extermination are wrong, no matter what, without qualification. Hence, the old problematic of objectivity and relativism, as we have called it, is now deepened and dramatized. After Auschwitz, no principles can be unconditional, and yet some must be. This paradox is the new crisis of objectivity that faces us.

Here we must say more about our current situation and the way in which this new crisis confronts us. Intellectual and cultural developments from the postwar period to the present have encouraged the view that all truths and principles are historically conditioned, interpretive, and perspectival. This is not the teaching of the Holocaust alone or even primarily; it is a widespread belief.

At least in part, views such as those of Richard Rorty and Charles Taylor, aside from the even more radical views associated with Jacques Derrida and Michel Foucault, occur at the intersection of two twentieth-century currents. I alluded to both earlier. One is the current that takes the proper perspective for philosophy and thought in general to be the perspective of the individual, experiencing, historically situated person. This current goes back at least to Husserl and Heidegger and further, to figures like Nietzsche, Dilthey, Hegel, and Kant. The other current, associated with this first one, is the postwar version of the late-nineteenth-century defense of the independence and character of the human sciences. Here Thomas Kuhn was a major voice; his influential book *The Structure of Scientific Revolutions,* originally published in 1962, posed a new way of look-

ing at the history of science and science itself and much else—
political theory, sociology, psychology, and history. According to
Kuhn, social and psychological factors play decisive roles in the character of human theorizing about nature, just as they do in our examination of human experience. Kuhn was responding to a narrow
conception of scientific investigation that emerged out of the school
of Vienna's logical positivism. This conception defined scientific
thinking in terms of strictly logical models of scientific inquiry and
theory construction. In response, Kuhn claimed that a great deal of
science is grounded in social and psychological factors and hence in
the very particular historical character of society, communities of
scientists, and the relevant culture. At roughly the same time, Isaiah
Berlin and Hayden White, in very different ways, were arguing that
disciplines such as history are distinct from the natural sciences insofar as they study human beings who are historically situated and
interpretive, whose worlds, lives, conduct, and beliefs have meaning
for them as interpretive and self-interpretive beings. Indeed, history
itself is historical and interpretive. By the late seventies, these currents had passed through an existential stage and taken the shape
of Alasdair MacIntyre's historical, neo-Nietzschean study of morali-
ties and Richard Rorty's historical and pragmatic account of the
historical character of modern philosophy. The new crisis of objectivity then manifested itself in a number of ways. MacIntyre took
on the challenge of showing how the historical developments of
traditions in moral thinking, epistemology, and much else were rational and neither arbitrary nor governed solely by power and political confrontation. Rorty, in a host of essays, tried to argue for a
resolution between the lack of foundations or groundedness and the
urgency of liberal attitudes about cruelty and suffering, what he
called the demand for "liberal irony." And Charles Taylor, in *Sources
of the Self,* tried to show how our current moral and political identity
incorporates components of different traditions, and that while it
is deeply historical, unstable, and changing, it also has certain values which, from our current perspective, it will not and should not
abandon.[24]

It is within this intellectual world that post-Holocaust Jewish religious self-reflection occurred. But while these philosophical developments, just mentioned, were largely driven by theoretical considerations, such as Kuhn's response to the positivist's model of scientific inquiry, the few prominent post-Holocaust Jewish theologians were not responding to intellectual issues primarily but rather to a horrific event, to their experience or the experience of others, and to memory and the traumas that would not go away. Nonetheless, their conclusions, while theological in content, are largely the same—the realization that we live in the time of a new crisis of objectivity, in which the *need* for unconditional principles is as great as the *reasons* for doubting their possibility are compelling. Or, to put their realization in historical terms, an honest and serious encounter with the death camps shows that continued Jewish existence, carried out by a retrieval of the Jewish past and its traditions, is as troubled and difficult as it is urgent and necessary.

We can see how this awareness of the crisis of objectivity emerges from theological encounters with the Holocaust if we look, if only briefly, at some of the major figures. Consider, for example, how two thinkers, Richard Rubenstein and Eliezer Berkovits, juxtapose the horrors of the death camps and the character of Nazi fascism with the traditional problem of evil. The issue here is one of approach and method. How each approaches the death camps and Nazi extermination is grounded in who they are and where each stands prior to his confrontation with Auschwitz.

A student of one of the great Halachic scholars of the twentieth century, Jehiel Jacob Weinberg, Berkovits was both an orthodox rabbi and a trained philosopher whose earliest work was on the Bible, classical rabbinic texts, and what might be called a traditional Jewish theology.[25] In an important set of essays, for example, Berkovits delivers a powerful critique of modern liberal Jewish thinkers from Cohen to Kaplan to Buber and Rosenzweig.[26] When Berkovits was first drawn to confront the Holocaust, following the Six Day War in 1967, he did so as a defender of traditional Jewish theology and of the power and significance of Jewish faith, even in the death camps.[27] For Berkovits, Biblical and rabbinic Judaism account for the existence of innocent suffering and moral evil by a doctrine of divine providence; according to that doctrine, God's charge to humankind, as a free and cooperative partner in the divine plan, is to bring moral and evaluative purpose to nature. The Jewish people are special witnesses to this task and this responsibility, but there are many who ignore or defy it. Such acts are not God's responsibility, although they are a possible outcome of His withholding of Divine Power and granting of human freedom, of His "hidden presence" or *hester panim,* God's hiding of His face. With freedom comes the possibility of the horrific and the morally reprehensible. Hence, the Holocaust is an act of human corruption. As Berkovits puts it, the appropriate question to ask about the Shoah is not where was God but rather where was man. Jewish history does not begin with the Holocaust; the death of one innocent child is no less a problem for Jewish theology than the murder of millions, and it is a problem for which there is, theologically speaking, an answer. Berkovits's approach, then, is to place the Holocaust within an existing intellectual framework; theologically speaking, there is nothing unique or distinctive about it.[28]

Rubenstein demurs. Brought up in a highly assimilated American Jewish world, Rubenstein moved to the Jewish Theological Seminary when he felt alienated by Reform Judaism. In the fifties he studied with Paul Tillich at the Harvard Divinity School and adopted an existential-naturalist understanding of religion, heavily influenced by Tillich and an array of modern figures from Freud and Sartre to Eliade, Dostoyevsky, and Camus. Moved by the death camps and their horror to worry about the continued vitality of traditional Jewish myths and beliefs grounded in the notion of an historical God, Rubenstein conceived of Judaism in terms of Tillich and Eliade. When in 1960 he first came to see the centrality of Auschwitz to Jewish life and Jewish belief, he viewed Judaism as a religion of nature with its symbolic and ritual structure organized to cope with human needs. In a sense, he may be seen to begin as Berkovits does, by confronting this intellectual paradigm—a benevolent, omnipotent, historically active God and the existence of suffering and evil in the world—with the events of Nazi fascism and the death camps. But whereas Berkovits's strategy is to display a solution to the problem and place the Holocaust within that solution, Rubenstein's approach is very different. To be sure, he proposes a type of answer, one that he appropriates from a German prelate but one that he thinks is indicative of a typical response, that the suffering and extermination of millions of Jews is part of God's plan and hence that somehow God is responsible and Hitler and his henchmen are God's implements. But Rubenstein does not stop at this point. He asks, can we live with this answer—indeed with this *type* of answer? He does not ask, is it reasonable or is it coherent or is it plausible. He asks, can we live with it, and his answer is that for him—and others like him—such an answer is repulsive; he calls it "obscene." And because it is, he claims, this shows—by a kind of existential *reductio ad absurdum* (or *modus tollens*)—that the problem of evil itself and the very conception of religion, Judaism, and God upon which it is founded must be abandoned. For Rubenstein and others like him, Judaism cannot be understood as a religion of history with a God of history, who acts in history and has an ongoing historical relationship with the Jewish people and with individual Jews. In its place and drawing on a multitude of sources, from Eliade and Tillich to Freud and Dostoyevsky and Sartre, Rubenstein proposes a kind of therapeutic Judaism—Judaism as understood by the social sciences, with rituals and myths tailored to help Jews cope with the traumas of birth, sickness, sexuality, and death that all of us, as human beings, must face.

By juxtaposing Berkovits and Rubenstein, then, we see that one issue raised by the Holocaust for Jewish belief and practice concerns the historicity of Jewish belief itself. Are even the most central Jewish affirmations historical and conditional or, as Berkovits would have it, do some concepts, theories, principles, or views resist modification but accommodate even the most horrific of events into their orbits? Here is the issue of objectivity raised not by general intellectual concerns with the historicity and hermeneutical character of all human experience but rather by the "seriousness" of a particular historical event. Berkovits and Rubenstein are haunted by the depth of the atrocity and the memories of its victims, by the evil itself. For them, the intellectual problem is subordinate to the human or existential one of living with this event and living in its shadow. If this one event is to be honestly encountered and if that means to appreciate it as "epoch-making," a rupture in our traditions and a test which every concept and principle must pass, then all our thinking is to this degree historically qualified.

It is a salient point that further thinkers, traditionalists like Irving Greenberg and more liberal thinkers like Emil Fackenheim, Protestants like A. Roy Eckardt and Catholics like David Tracy, side with Rubenstein on this matter, all the while realizing that the same depth of horror that requires that we not cordon off theological beliefs as too sacred to be changed, revised, or even refuted, *also* requires our unqualified opposition. This feature is the other dimension of the paradox posed by Auschwitz, that while honesty about this event requires considering all beliefs and principles qualified in its wake, it also requires that some beliefs and principles be treated as fixed, firm, and non-negotiable, precisely those that oppose the "forces of evil," the horrific assault on human dignity and human life. *If unqualified or unconditional principles after Auschwitz are impossible, they are also necessary.*

Perhaps the best place to see both poles of this crisis, both sides of this paradox, is in Emil Fackenheim's *To Mend the World.* Fackenheim is one of the most articulate and philosophically serious of the "new" Jewish theologians, the existential theologians, of the postwar period. Having studied classics in the *Stadtgymnasium* in Halle, he matriculated at the Hochschule in Berlin in 1935, his commitment to the rabbinate motivated by the rise of Nazism, the threat to Jews and Judaism, and his sense of urgency about the need to rethink the nature of Judaism. After *Kristallnacht,* he was incarcerated in Sachsenhausen and eventually fled to Scotland and then Canada, where he entered a doctoral program in Philosophy at the University of Toronto. Fackenheim received his degree in 1945, with a dissertation on the doctrine of substance in the philosophy of the Islamic sect, the Ikwan Sufa, having already taken a position as a congregational Reform rabbi in Hamilton, Ontario, two years before. By 1948 he was writing essays on contemporary Jewish theology, the primacy of faith and revelation, and the inadequacies of religious naturalism. But for nearly two decades he resisted any encounter with the Nazi evil, with the death camps, the atrocity, and the attempt to exterminate Judaism and the Jewish people. In 1966 and then, most vividly in 1967, he broke that silence.[29] *To Mend the World*, first published in 1982, is the high point of three decades of books and essays that attempt to clarify what a post-Holocaust Jewish life and thought might be.

In the central chapter of that work Fackenheim attempts to expose the inadequacy of our conceptual schemes and theories to grasp and explain what happened. The event outstrips our categories, our explanations, and our understanding. At the same time, Fackenheim tries to show that the only kind of authentic response is to resist and oppose. A single movement of thought carries Fackenheim from an honest encounter with the event, its criminals, and its victims to the conditionality of all our thinking to the unconditionality of opposition. Successful or not, Fackenheim's reasoning exhibits both poles of the paradox of objectivity as we have described it; whether or not the Jewish thinker can resolve the problem is one thing, but face it one must.

Step by step, Fackenheim considers the agents, the crimes, and the victims, trying always to explain and understand what happened and why it happened, and in every case, no matter how careful our examination, how probing our analysis, the phenomena resist intellectual satisfaction. This is Fackenheim's first claim, one sure to be controversial and provocative but at the same time one terribly important: that the evil of the Nazi Holocaust in the end resists being intellectually domesticated. Fackenheim extends Rubenstein's existential repulsiveness, one shared by Irving Greenberg and Roy Eckardt and others. In the end, as he is fond of quoting Hans Jonas, in Auschwitz "much more is real than is possible."[30]

Here then is the conditionality of all theological, psychological, political, and such thinking; all our views are qualified. But there is more. As the mind thinks through the agents, the crimes, and the victims, it finally arrives at a whole that is larger than its parts, a whole of horror, and when it grasps that whole, it both confronts it

and recoils from it, and in recoiling it realizes the need to oppose
it, a need that the religious Jew, tentatively and with uncertainty,
might eventually ground in the traditional Jewish notion of divine
command. Here, then, is the second pole of the paradox, so to
speak, the necessity of opposition, the unconditionality of some
principles in the face of the horror. Earlier, in the period just before
and after the Six Day War in 1967, Fackenheim had called this awareness and its content a 614th commandment, not to give Hitler any
posthumous victories. By 1982, Fackenheim rarely used this formulation any longer—to call the imperative a "commandment" and to
ground it in God is, even for the believer, a hope and not a *fait
accompli*—but the gist of it remained as the sense of necessary opposition that theological and philosophical thought realizes as one
outcome of its attempt to understand and cope with the horrors of
Auschwitz.

But, in *To Mend the World,* there is more. Fackenheim asks: if
there is for us an imperative to resist Nazi purposes and to oppose
the legacy of inhumanity and evil, what makes us think that it is an
imperative that can be satisfied? Modern moral thinkers, secular
and religious, have regularly worried about the commensurability of
moral obligation and human capacity. Kant had argued that ought
implies can, that the existence of the moral law is reason for believing that human beings are free to perform it. Thinkers like Barth
and Rosenzweig had worried that a divine command, the burden of
the infinite on the finite, threatened to annihilate our humanity and
not enrich it. Hence, they claimed that the revelation itself incorporated not only demand as a gift of grace but also the human freedom to receive it and respond to it and that all of this was an act
of divine love. Fackenheim, in a sense, had considered either one of
these acceptable in 1968; by 1982 neither seems to be so. In their
place, he seeks some ground of the possibility of a post-Holocaust
Jewish life that, whatever its grounds, can be lived; if there is an
imperative to oppose hatred and inhumanity, what makes us think
that we can perform it? Only one thing will do, the actuality of
resistance to Nazi atrocity in the event itself, performed consciously

and with a reflective sense that the resistance is in response to a command of some sort. Fackenheim quotes, as support, the testimony of a Polish victim, Pelagia Lewinska:

> At the outset the living places, the ditches, the mud, the piles of excrement behind the blocks, had appalled me with their horrible filth. . . . And then I saw the light! I saw that it was not a question of disorder or lack of organization but that, on the contrary, a very thoroughly considered conscious idea was in the back of the camp's existence. They had condemned us to die in our own filth, to drown in mud, in our own excrement. They wished to abase us, to destroy our human dignity, to efface every vestige of humanity, to return us to the level of wild animals, to fill us with horror and contempt toward ourselves and our fellows.
>
> But from the instant that I grasped the motivating principle . . . it was as if I had been awakened from a dream . . . I felt under orders to live . . . And if I did die in Auschwitz, it would be as a human being, I would hold on to my dignity. I was not going to become the contemptible, disgusting brute my enemy wished me to be . . . And a terrible struggle began which went on day and night.[31]

What, then, is the collective outcome of post-Holocaust Jewish thought? It is that after the Holocaust, Jews are faced with a twofold challenge. The first is to take Auschwitz seriously by accepting the historicity and conditionality of all Jewish beliefs and principles; nothing is as it was. All our concepts, our categories, and our understanding must be rethought, and hence, in principle, all must undergo revision and change, and will again and again. The second challenge, however, is to recognize that honesty about Auschwitz also requires honest opposition and that this opposition involves taking Judaism and the God of Judaism seriously. Essential to Nazism was the murderous assault on humanity and human dignity and also the murderous assault on Judaism, body and soul. Hence, a serious encounter with the Holocaust points to a response with some unconditionality about it, a firm and committed opposition to all the forces that assail human dignity and worth and a committed defense of all that is valuable and decent, and of Judaism and its purposes, and, for those who can do so, of the relationship between the Jewish people and God.

Jewish post-Holocaust thought, then, teaches us that recovery of the Jewish past should and can occur; that to take the Holocaust seriously and also to take Judaism, indeed *God* seriously, one must realize that, while all principles and all beliefs might some day be revised or rejected, there are some *now* that one holds to be unconditional. And as a Jew, one realizes too that such principles or beliefs are binding; we perform them because we must.

Interim Obligation and a Life of Active Waiting

Where, however, does this "must" come from? Or, in the terms we used earlier, what is the ground of the objectivity of these principles or beliefs? Part of the task of a post-Holocaust Jewish life is to determine what shape the life is to take, what one must do. But part too is to recognize that when that task is performed, the outcome is not a set of recommendations or opportunities or suggestions but rather a picture of what one ought to do as a Jew in America at this moment and as long as one can foresee. For us, moreover, as people reflecting upon this process, it is also important to identify, if we can, where the locus or ground of that obligatoriness or commandedness lies. If the other tasks are difficult, this may be the most difficult of all.

In the years before and after World War I, among artists, poets, theologians, and social critics, there was a sense that the only way to be secure against the threats of relativism and nihilism was to find the ground of orientation in transcendence, for this alone brought with it unconditionality, timelessness, and generality. For these intellectuals, reason had its limits; it was conditional in a variety of ways. And nothing else—not nature or some aspect of nature—was sufficient to ground objectivity. Today, however, such a leap to transcendence seems glib and facile. Where, then, should we turn?

First, there are many reasons for rejecting relativism. As I indicated earlier, some argue against relativism as self-refuting and therefore incoherent. How can the relativist claim that all beliefs, norms, or values, in meaning or truth, are relative to a cultural group, historical periods, or individuals? Is it not self-contradictory for the relativist to claim that his or her own relativist view is not relatively meaningful and true but rather absolutely so? Others probe more deeply. They may distinguish between the everyday or first-order beliefs to which the relativist view applies and the relativist view itself. What the relativist claims, they acknowledge, is that all first-order beliefs are relative to persons, groups, or periods with respect to what they mean and their truth, but this is not so of the relativist view itself, which is not an ordinary or first-order belief. Still, they ask, how can the relativist achieve the standpoint from which the relativist view—or any such view, for example, a skeptical view—might be made? If we, as persons, are always embedded in historically determined situations, with all their particular and variable features, how can one make any comprehensive or global claims about the meaning and truth of beliefs? Are not all of our beliefs conditioned and situated? Is the distinction between ordinary beliefs and second-order ones artificial and fatuous? Or, if such claims are the result of what we might call "philosophical" reflection, does this not show the irrelevance or artificiality of such reflection? Does it not show that philosophy, as the venue of such claims and problems, is a distortion rather than an understanding of human experience and human existence?

Such thinking has led many to dispense with "global" relativism and associated views as either incoherent or irrelevant. Embedded human existence is unavoidable and no complete transcendence of it is possible. Some have argued this way about the first-person or subjective point of view and its unavoidability, although this has not prevented them from acknowledging the human propensity to try to overcome it, to arrive at some kind of objectivity with regard to our understanding of natural events, human actions, beliefs, and more. One lesson to be learned, then, from such a proposal may be that once global relativism is jettisoned in favor of a recognition of our situatedness, the outcome may be a kind of middle road between such global relativism and objectivity or realism.

But even this kind of view may be too much to hope for. After all, what does such a view or what can such a view say about our beliefs, judgments, and principles? Surely not that their meaning and truth are always situated and conditioned. Does this middle road, too, fail, since even it cannot say anything coherent and clear about our situatedness, on the one hand, and the objectivity of our beliefs and principles, on the other?

And yet, from our particular perspective, embedded in time, place, and culture, we do make universal judgments and we do articulate firm and fixed principles. We do debate with one another; we engage in group discussions; we make collective decisions. Even if our perspective is historically situated and embedded and even if we realize that beliefs and principles mean things to us that they did not mean to others in medieval Spain or Eastern Europe in the nineteenth century or Germany during the Weimar period, nonetheless we have a sense of commitment, permanence, and firmness about much that we believe and much that we do. In our everyday lives as Jews and as people living in early-twenty-first-century America, we do act in terms of some notion of objectivity and of unconditional obligation. There are truths and duties that are present to us as independent of our particular will and our choice. Indeed, we can and often do make a distinction of just this kind, between beliefs we hold for personal reasons and beliefs we hold for common reasons that are independent of idiosyncrasy and personal peculiarities. We have an operative understanding of what philosophers call "agent neutral" reasons, and that operative understanding is one reason for thinking that objectivity of some sort is part of our lives.

In our everyday lives, objectivity gives rise to several sorts of investigation and several sorts of questions. One is about precise content: what exactly should we believe? How exactly should we act? What should we do? Normally, in our everyday lives, this is where we begin. Often—not always, of course—we assume that there is an "ought" about things, and what we want to determine is its content. With regard to privacy and e-mail, for example, what ought we to hold; what sort of policy should there be? With regard to euthanasia, the physician's role, and the responsibility of family, what should we do? How should we deal with the terminally ill and the use of extraordinary life-support systems? But there are times when we are not even certain about this assumption; this gives rises to the second sort of question: is there an "ought" in this situation? Should we be bound? Is there a right or wrong? Is this a situation where the notion of obligation or duty applies? Or, alternatively, is this a situation that calls for a decision based on taste or personal preference or likes and dislikes? Finally, there is a third sort of question. Even if we agree that there is an "ought" that applies here, what grounds the "ought" or provides the imperative force behind the obligation? This question is about justification or explanation; it is about why, not why we should do this particular thing but rather why there is a bindingness to this particular duty or obligation, why it is a duty or obligation rather than something else.

If there is, in Jewish life today, a crisis of objectivity, with regard to beliefs and to actions, then it is a crisis that is felt in all three ways. Once we appreciate this complexity, moreover, we can see that it might be possible to answer one or more of these questions about objectivity without answering all three and that the order of our investigation and our answering might not be the same in every case. Most often, what stimulates our worries, our deliberation, and our discussion is the question of particular content: what, in this situation, should we do? The answers to the other questions seem tacit. If we are traditional Jews, we assume that the belief or principle is binding because it is grounded in tradition and God. And if we are liberal Jews, we assume that in the end what makes any belief or principle binding for each of us is our accepting it for ourselves and just as often we find it easy to treat such self-determination as not a form of determination at all, as not really binding or obligatory but rather optional because voluntary.

But the issue about relativism and objectivity and the formulation of these three questions may, in fact, be leading us astray. Underlying this picture is an assumption about ourselves and our lives. In order to see more clearly where we stand, we may need to modify that assumption and the picture it supports. Let me call the assumption "atomism." It is deeply embedded in Western philosophy, theology, and culture. According to atomism, the nature of things is to be precisely bounded, isolated entities. Once we understand what these entities contain and how, we are able to ask how each is related to others, how they interact or exclude interaction, and so forth. Atomism applies to people, just as it applies to other natural objects. Hence, if we want to understand how a person understands the world around her by sensory experience, we ask about her sensory capabilities, what sensation is, what sensory representation is all about, and what the objects of sensation are. We then ask what it means to say that sensation is true or accurate as a way of understanding the world or something in it, e.g., a flower or a building or a sunset. Atomism similarly underlies many attempts to understand our beliefs, our desires, and our moral principles. We begin by assuming separation and self-containment and try to clarify these phenomena by understanding how two or more isolated entities are related. Objectivity, on this picture, is about the relationship between a person and something, say, the population of Mexico City. Some might say that my belief about the population of Mexico City is relative to me, my capacities, my context, and so on, in a variety of ways both what my belief means and its truth. Others might say that the meaning and especially the truth about the population of Mexico City—say, what it is—is fixed absolutely and completely by one and only one thing, the population of Mexico City. The same model applies to principles or rules, statements about what we ought to do, although in this case the issue is not one of accuracy but rather one of concern or deference or relevance or some other such relationship.

There is something very artificial about this picture and the atomism that underlies it, an artificiality and indeed distortedness that has been recognized by many, especially early-twentieth-century European intellectuals from Buber and Rosenzweig to Martin Heidegger and Emmanuel Levinas. In fact, in our everyday lives, we do not live as isolated atoms; rather, from the outset of our lives, we live in networks of relatedness or, as Buber put it after the early 1920s, we live in the between, in relation to the world, to the things around us—from natural objects to artifacts to cultural objects to persons. Our mode of being is always within such networks. If we want to understand what a relationship should be, we must look at all the things it is and has been, for these tell us what both the related things contribute to the totality of their relationship. Hence, to make a great leap, if we want to understand Jewish obligation, we need to observe and understand how Jews both today and in the past have been related to other Jews, to practices and principles, to the Jewish community, to others, to God, and more, to see where, when, and how the sense of duty tied them together, if it did. In short, objectivity arises out of experience; it is not imposed a priori upon it.

For modern Jews, then, to deal with the crisis of objectivity, one must start not with theory but rather with life. The goal is to understand what the Jew's relationship to the Jewish past is and should be, what the relationship to Jewish texts, tradition, and learning is, what the relationship is to communities, and ultimately to God. As for what objectivity means to people and where its grounds lie—these things are not abstract intellectual problems. Rather, they will arise out of lived experience with communities, texts, traditions, rituals, and indeed with God. People do not live as isolated atoms; nor are these realities isolated entities. The issue is not how intellectually two independent entities are related in terms of that which is authoritative for the other. Rather, people live in relation; and what each—individuals and texts, individuals and communities, and individuals and God—contribute to their lives' having a binding sense of direction and meaning arises out of lived experience. This much of Rosenzweig must be recovered: the proper place to begin is with life. What constitutes objectivity and where the objective grounds lie are things that will emerge out of a context of lived relationships and not independently of it. As I just put it, these issues are not about how, a priori, we must conceive the issue of dependency between two basically isolated entities; rather, it is how we understand the nature of the dependency that emerges from a set of lived relationships.

What this means specifically is that facing the problem of objectivity is not a matter of seeking a theoretical justification upon which all can agree, nor is it a matter of debating theological issues about covenant or ethnic identity. It is, rather, a matter of going about the business of confronting situations that demand debate and discussion, trying to decide what to do and whether or not to have a principle or policy about it, and then to wait. For life makes some demands upon us, which cannot be delayed, while other issues—often those of justification—can wait or indeed *must* wait. It may be that for some, grounding Jewish obligation in divine will and hence taking all such obligations as *mitzvot* (command-ments) in a very literal sense are very important results; for them, this may seem to be a goal for all Jewish life. But for now, we may agree on what to do without agreeing on why, and that may have to be sufficient. For more, we may have to wait.

My proposal for contemporary Judaism in America, then, is a life of deliberation and action that is also a life of waiting, but the kind of waiting I have in mind is very distinctive. Let me distin-guish between two kinds of waiting; to do so, I return to early-twentieth-century culture. To many, Kafka's famous parable "Before the Law," written in December 1914 and published the next year, is a parable about waiting. The man from the country encounters the guard before the gate to the Law and is forbidden entrance; he ques-tions, peers beyond the gate that is ajar, and then settles into wait-ing, for days, months, and then years—indeed a lifetime. He loses attention of the Law and focuses exclusively on the gatekeeper; the man waits, does nothing, and grows old. Eventually he dies, a life lived and wasted, some would say, in the shadow of the abyss be-tween truth and human existence. This is an estranged waiting, a waste, perhaps even pointless.

But there is another kind of waiting, a Jewish life that is both active and cautious, a life of doing and waiting. Such a life was anticipated by a Weimar secular Jew, albeit for different reasons. In 1922 Siegfried Kracauer published a short essay called "Those Who Wait." In it he described the contemporary professional or intellec-tual, living a life of loneliness, of alienation, and of despair over the loss of meaning and a connection to the absolute. Kracauer also outlined available options for such a person—among them the skep-tical denial of any possible reconnection with the absolute or tran-scendent and the facile choice of faith. But he also pictured a third option, which he recommended. He called it "waiting," but it is what we might call an "engaged waiting." Kracauer also described it as "a hesitant openness" which "consists of tense activity and engaged self-preparation. . . . a long path . . . which leads to life in the religious sphere, to the religious word, and even to the closeness between men that is based on a communal belief." It is something that "must be lived" and is not grounded in some a priori belief or theory or ideology; "what is at stake . . . is an attempt to shift the focus from the theoretical self to the self of the entire human being." Here, then, is a coping with the threat of nihilism that is neither a confident choice nor utter passivity. It is rooted in life, in commitments and action, but it is also cautious, sober, realistic, and in its own way anticipatory. It is this kind of engaged waiting that I propose as a Jewish response to the crisis of objectivity today.[32]

Recently many thinkers have tried to argue that objectivity can be found in nature or rationality and that we should not seek a transcendence that is unnecessary and illusory. To many, science—evolutionary biology, cognitive psychology, and so forth—shows exactly why we desire the things we do, act as we do, and more, but these attempts may not be compelling to all, nor are the attempts to ground principles in something like the rationality that we treat as common to all.[33] Our situation is not one of consensus; it is less determinate. Emil Fackenheim is fond of quoting a passage from Nietzsche's autobiographical *Ecce Homo* that Buber often cited: "One takes and does not ask who gives."[34] Given where we stand and who we are, our task may be to recognize the phenomenon of demandedness, of being bound, required, and to make every effort to determine what indeed our duties are. At least for now, we may differ over what objectivity is and what lies behind it, if anything at all. There is objectivity; we live with it and cannot live without it, even if we cannot now agree on what grounds it. Some of us will think that objectivity lies in our choices, that ultimate authority is ours alone. Others will think that it rests with the past, with tradition, or with the culture or ethos of the Jewish people, or with our local communal or congregational decisions, or with the decisions of our leaders, our rabbis, local and national and even international.

Others still will think that to be genuinely Jewish such authority, such groundedness, must rest on God alone and on our relationship to God. We stand in different places; our confidences and our doubts differ; what is possible for one of us may not be possible for others. Still, if recent Jewish thought is a good guide, we live in a time when, as Emil Fackenheim has said, the *immediate* challenge may not be to know the one true God but rather to recognize those gods that are false.[35] And this challenge means that as Jews our lives do have a direction, an orientation, a purpose; we need to find it. Only the future will reveal if, along the way, at some point, we may too come to understand and perhaps even to agree upon its ground.

2

REVELATION, LANGUAGE, AND THE SEARCH FOR TRANSCENDENCE

Revelation and Access to the Transcendent: The Problem Today

In recent decades, in America and throughout the world, there has been a resurgence of *religious sensibility*. This process includes a return to ritual practice, a widespread interest in religious texts, and a surge of religious activity in politics. The latter has not been only an American phenomenon, marked by the growth of the Christian right and of religious and quasi-religious issues as central political chess pieces; it has also manifested itself powerfully in places such as Northern Ireland, Iraq, and Israel.[1] Among the paradigmatic scholarly symbols of this intense interaction between the religious and the political, for example, is Clifford Geertz's famous essay "Deep Play: Notes on the Balinese Cockfight."[2]

One of the most important features of this interest and activity concerning religion, however, is that it is not primarily about religious ideas or religious beliefs in any clear sense. Rather, it is about that aspect of religion we call "sensibility." It is about basic attitudes, feelings, and the ethos of religious life and all that it involves.

In Western culture, certainly in America, this revival of the religious sensibility does, however, have an intellectual dimension. It registers in some serious questions that at one time were dealt with in a totally secular fashion but now, as for most of the history of Western thought and culture, have regained a religious cast. One such question, for example, is about moral and political purposes. Can reason serve adequately to ground our values? Or can nature? Is it possible for us to go about our moral and political business without acknowledging some transcendent ground? This is the theme of an interesting book by Fergus Kerr entitled *Immortal Longings,* in which Kerr, a Dominican philosopher at Blackfriars in Edinburgh, considers how a number of twentieth-century intellectuals—including Martha Nussbaum, Karl Barth, Martin Heidegger, Iris Murdoch, Stanley Cavell, and Charles Taylor—have dealt with this very question.[3]

For Jewish life in America, this religious revival began in the late sixties and early seventies. It was stimulated by the growth of black nationalism in the civil rights movement and, after the Six Day War, by the way in which black leadership and the new left turned on Israel, thereby alienating and isolating many Jewish intellectuals and other Jews. One result was a Jewish shift to a politics of identity and to a search for new content for the sense of Jewish solidarity.[4] This was the period of the emphasis on worship and the intimacy of small groups of the *chavurah* movement, which eventually even influenced synagogue life, of the flourishing of Jewish folk-rock liturgy, and of a return to ritual in Reform Judaism. It also was at the leading edge of a very selective Jewish politics with regard to Israel and a slow but sure effort to mitigate the importance of the memory of the Holocaust and to decenter the Holocaust in Jewish identity, one that has had to accommodate to a boom in Holocaust publications and even to the ritual incorporation of the Holocaust memory in liturgy.[5] This renewal movement occurred simultaneously with and interacted with the rise of Jewish feminism; it also blossomed, in the eighties and nineties, into the movement called "Jewish spirituality," a Jewish version of the new age and metaphysics rage that has been very much a part of pop culture for the past decades.

For a number of reasons, these trends raise a serious problem for Jewish thought and self-understanding. Many of these developments focus on religious experience and religious ritual practice. These trends invariably point to God, the divine, and especially to questions about our access to transcendence or our experience of God. Since the trends first emerged as part of an effort to reinvigorate Jewish worship and celebrations, to bring a sense of elevation, personal fulfillment, and joy to Jewish prayer, they have also drawn into their orbit a widespread interest in the Kabbalah and Jewish mysticism and with it mystical terminology, mythological storytelling, and mystical-style meditative practices. In traditional Jewish terminology, the conglomerate raises questions about divine revelation and about the relation between God's presence and human experience.

I should point out, as a caveat, that while these recent trends in Jewish life *should* point to the notion of divine revelation and compel us to a careful reconsideration of it, I do not see much activity of this sort. Most people seem happy to go about seeking spiritual fulfillment, deepening in some psychologically effective way the experience of worship and ritual celebration, and appropriating mystical vocabulary and style without ever asking what all of this means with regard to the human relationship with God. This is hardly surprising. Rarely in our lives do we venture into the foreboding domains of clarification and justification; we regularly are satisfied to manage to live with some sense of fulfillment, principle, and dignity without asking how it is possible and why it is necessary. But since synagogues, communities, and national organizations seem to be turning these recent tendencies into programs and policies, they now take on the character of an understanding of Jewish destiny and Jewish purpose. And if that is to be the case, then we certainly ought to seek to understand them, their foundations, and their significance for our understanding of what Judaism is and ought to be. Revelation is a very traditional Jewish notion, and we should want to understand that notion for ourselves, in a way that is meaningful and acceptable. Moreover, if our age is one in which we struggle as well with the role of transcendence in our quest for objectivity, then our access to that transcendence is of vital concern. Is there such access and how does it occur? Are we talking about mystical ecstasy, religious experience of a rational kind, or something very different?

Revelation: Buber's Response to the Traditional Views

The early twentieth century, from about 1910 to the 1930s, was an extraordinarily rich period of reflection on this theme. For philosophers and psychologists, poets and religious theologians, the idea of *experience* was the subject of important and deep speculation. At one time or another, for many, that speculation came to be focused on the experience of God and the relation between the divine and the human. To be sure, this period of exciting reflection did not occur in a vacuum, either historical or intellectual, but it does rise above its surroundings as a moment of supreme and enduring importance.

In the eighteenth century, the blending of the new science and philosophy led to great intellectual systems that we associate with the Enlightenment and the preeminence of reason and rational thought. One outcome for the idea of revelation was the conviction that our knowledge of God, His relation to nature, to humankind and to morality, should be understood as a rational achievement; natural theology sealed this conviction in arguments for God's existence and providence, grounded in our understanding of nature and our knowledge of the metaphysics which supported that scientific edifice. Kant's critique of traditional metaphysics was in part a critique of this natural theology and hence of the style of religious thought and philosophy that someone like Moses Mendelssohn found so congenial. But when Kant himself located the role for God and religion within morality, as the ground for the *Summum Bonum,* this was in essence a variation on the rationalism of his predecessors and hence on the commitment to revelation or knowledge of God wholly had by rational thought.

Even in his own day there were fideists who opposed Kant's rational treatment of the human relationship with God with a conception of faith that was non-rational. I am thinking of figures such as Johann Casper Lavater, Johann Georg Hamann, and especially Friedrich Jacobi.[6] Already then they anticipated the Romantic reaction of the nineteenth century that we associate with figures such as Schleiermacher, the Schlegels, and Novalis, and the elevation of feeling and emotion as the primary vehicles for the human relationship with God. The manifesto of this anti-rationalist response to Kant and the Enlightenment conception of the rationality of revelation is surely Schleiermacher's lectures *On Religion,* but we associate this response generally with all the Romantics with religious convictions and with many others in the century.[7]

By the time Martin Buber came on the scene, from 1904 to 1913, with his profound interest in mystical, ecstatic experience, his appropriation of Hasidism as a model of Jewish renewal, and his commitment to myth, the nineteenth century had seen both the rational and non-rational strands continue throughout the century. One strand assimilated revelation to reason, in a Kantian or Hegelian style, and the other conceived of revelation as some kind of non-rational, non-cognitive access to the divine. They fought with each other and even, occasionally, interacted, and both were, of course, subjected to the withering critique of revelation that we associate with the names of Feuerbach, Marx, Nietzsche, and later Freud.

Within the Jewish tradition, Buber's conception of revelation as direct, intuitive, non-cognitive, and ecstatic took shape as a reaction to three views of revelation that had predominated within Judaism. One was the tradition, going back to Maimonides, Saadia, and others, according to which revelation occurred through human reason. Throughout the Middle Ages, when Judaism and Aristotelian science and philosophy came into conflict, one common outcome was a view of revelation and prophecy conceived as an accomplishment of reason, especially scientific rationality. A second view held that revelation was the individual and communal reception of Torah, of a divine voice that communicated literally the word of God either in spirit or in fact, to Moses, the prophets, and then designated heirs of the mantel of authoritative receptivity. This view was canonized within the rabbinic tradition as the doctrine of the two Torahs, the Written and the Oral Torah [*Torah sheb'al peh* and *Torah shebichtav*]. A final view was that the revelation itself was linguistic but somehow shrouded in the mists of Biblical antiquity, that it was then embedded in the commentaries and later rabbinic reflections, and that contemporary access to it could be had only mediated through the interpretive tradition. This view was enshrined within both the rabbinic texts and within the Kabbalah. What all of these views shared as a common assumption was the notion of mediation; ongoing revelation was an indirect exposure of the divine to the human through some agency—reason, special experience, language, or some combination of these.[8]

Buber had an affinity for the experiential side of mysticism and for the fideist reaction to modern rationalism. Indebted to Kierkegaard and his reaction to the Hegelian tradition, he turned to a conception of revelation as direct divine-human relation. Revelation or faith was, to be sure, grounded in human experience, but it was a larger notion. Faith incorporated the entire life of the believing Jew as he or she sought to respond in language and in action, in myth and in ritual, to the experience of revelation. The believer's experience confirmed or transformed the significance of the pristine encounter between God and the people of Israel, the earliest response to which is recorded in the Biblical story. For Buber, even in his early or mystical period, the revelation of God to the Jewish people was not a revelation of a content as much as the revelation of a presence. This presence made a demand, called for a decision. To be sure, prior to World War I he associated the moment of revelation, on the human side, with ecstatic experience, a view he would later abandon. Nonetheless, the key was that this revelation was not for him a matter of content, rational or linguistic, but rather a matter of demand and decision. In his introductory essay to his collection of mystical testimonies, published in 1909, Buber describes this ecstatic experience this way:

> One cannot burden the general run of occurrences with this experience [of ecstasy]; one does not dare to lay it upon his own poor I . . . ; so one hangs it on God. And what one thinks, feels and dreams about God then enters into his ecstasies, pours itself out upon them in a shower of images and sounds, and creates around the experience of

unity a multiform mystery. . . . The ecstatic cannot say the unsayable. He says the other thing—images, dreams, visions—not unity. He speaks, he must speak, because the Word burns in him.[9]

The center of revelation, for Buber, was God, and in this respect, his theological posture shared something with that of Karl Barth, Paul Tillich, Rudolf Bultmann, and Friedrich Gogarten, whose affirmations of the centrality of God and divine revelation were responses, albeit diverse, to the liberal theology of the nineteenth century, with its focus on human experience and human history.[10] Buber was moved by his reading of Nietzsche, his sensitivity to Hasidism and other mystical testimonies, and his voluntaristic understanding of a Jewish renewal that needed to replace formalism, law, and a sense of subordination with vitality and dynamism. Barth was motivated by the war and the liberal optimism that fed the infatuation with the war; Bultmann was compelled by the inadequacies of Biblical scholarship, the false association of God with moral goodness, and the mistaken notion of sin. Tillich's painful and disturbing experience on the front lines led him to socialism and to a placid optimism about human experience and its capabilities. While these thinkers did differ, then, they shared a good deal. Buber preceded them and in a sense anticipated them; man is man and God is God, and if they are to meet, it is up to God to initiate the encounter and to provide humankind with direction and purpose.

Within Jewish circles, Buber's conception had its adherents, but it also led to three developments that are of special interest to us. One is through Buber's own development and his conception of dialogue, of the I-Thou encounter between the human and the Eternal Thou, the divine. Buber's classic formulation is given in Part Three of *I and Thou:*

> Extended, the lines of relationships intersect in the eternal Thou.
> Every single Thou is a glimpse of that. Through every single Thou the basic word addresses the eternal Thou. . . . [Each Thou] attains perfection solely in the immediate relationship to the Thou that in accordance with its nature cannot become an It.
> One does not find God if one remains in the world; one does not find God if one leaves the world. . . . Of course, God is "the wholly

Other"; but he is also the wholly same: the wholly present . . . the mystery of the obvious that is closer to me than my own I.

What is . . . the primal phenomenon, present in the here and now, of what we call revelation? It is man's emerging from the moment of the supreme encounter, being no longer the same as he was when entering into it. The moment of encounter is not a "living experience" (*Erlebnis*) that stirs in the receptive soul and blissfully rounds itself out: something happens to man. . . . The man who steps out of the essential act of pure relation has something More in his being, something new has grown there of which he did not know before and for whose origin he lacks any suitable words. . . .

Man receives, and what he receives is not a "content" but a presence, a presence as strength. This presence . . . includes three elements. . . . First, [it makes] life heavy with meaning . . . second: [the meaning] is guaranteed. Nothing, nothing can henceforth be meaningless. . . . [The meaning] does not wish to be interpreted by us—for that we lack the ability—only to be done by us. This comes third: it is not the meaning of "another life" but that of this life. . . . The meaning we receive can be put to the proof in action only by each person in the uniqueness of his being and in the uniqueness of his life. No prescription can lead us to the encounter, and none leads from it.[11]

By the early twenties, then, Buber remained committed to the immediacy of the divine-human encounter but had jettisoned his infatuation with mysticism, which he had come to see as an indefensible abnegation of the individual's integrity and worth.

A second development is through Franz Rosenzweig and his adoption of a notion of revelation as orientation. A third is through Gershom Scholem and Walter Benjamin and their linguistic conception of revelation that took shape in direct opposition to Buber and his disciples. For our purposes, we can focus on Rosenzweig first and then turn to Scholem and Benjamin.

Rosenzweig and Beyond

Revelation is a reciprocal event. God and human agency collaborate; the divine reveals and the human receives. Revelation succeeds only when both occur. But, one might ask, how can both occur, for after all the divine is divine and the human human? How can the absolute reveal itself, communicate, touch the relative and limited, and still be absolute? And how can the conditional and finite receive the absolute and survive the encounter?

One solution to this paradox of revelation is mystical union. Not only is the human in touch with the divine; it also achieves unity and wholeness in the very act of encounter. But it does so—the self accomplishes unification—only by grabbing one horn of the dilemma. The divine remains divine, but the human does not, as it were, remain human. The self dissolves into the godhead; distinctness and limitation are overcome. The divine and the human come into direct, unmediated encounter but only by means of the sacrifice of the human.

Franz Rosenzweig, so far as I can tell, never leaned in the mystical direction—although others, from Georg Simmel to Buber, Georg Lukács, Ernst Bloch, and Gustav Landauer, did. Rosenzweig's response to the need for revelation and transcendence and the challenges of historicism, relativism, and nihilism was, in a sense, to grab hold of both horns, to hold together the divine and the human, to argue for the integrity of each and to accept their ultimate incommensurability, and yet to remain with the immediacy of their encounter. Buber, in his conception of dialogue, came to agree to something similar. Both started with the need for human orientation, for the groundedness of value and direction; both recognized the limitations of reason, nature, and history. Value, purpose, and meaning must be grounded in what transcends nature and humankind. But how? Only by means of an act of divine grace. Humankind cannot bring about the divine directedness; it can receive it, respond to it, and even need it. But God and God alone can enter history and nature, open itself to human acknowledgment, and call forth human response. In the spirit of such a view, in 1913, Rosenzweig became a convert to Eugen Rosenstock's notion of revelation as an event of orientation, which he took to be a decisive response to the problems of relativism and nihilism. It was this view that he developed from 1917 to 1918 into a full-blown account of what revelation is, how it occurs, and what it means to humankind.[12]

Rosenzweig gives an especially clear formulation of it in two comments on poems of Jehuda Halevi, written between 1922 and 1924:

> Revelation is experience and event. Genuine experience only, because
> and when it also has been event, genuine event only, because and when
> it can become experience again and again. . . . [13]
>
> Does God or does the human take the first step? That is a real
> question. . . . The real question arises because the human always
> senses his own lack of power whenever he stands before God, and
> thus necessarily must await and request the first step from God. And
> yet at the same time he hears that which he cannot help but hear:
> that God demands the first step from him, from the human. No
> theory can get away from this, neither one that seeks to discredit the
> demanding voice of God that is heard, nor one that seeks to discredit
> the perceived lack of power as a deception of Satan. . . . [14]

As these passages indicate, for Rosenzweig revelation is immediate,
a disclosing, orienting confrontation that is received by persons and
calls out to them, orients their lives. Structurally and metaphorically,
it is, in a sense, linguistic or akin to the linguistic, for it is a temporal
act of direct communication. But revelation contains no human language as its content. Revelation is an event of—akin to—address
and response; yet it employs no concepts, words, or expressions.
What language there is in the orbit of revelation occurs before and
after, most notably as one mode of response to the orienting directedness itself.

Buber and Rosenzweig, independently at first and then together,
developed their views concerning revelation and language roughly
from 1915, through the decade and then throughout the Weimar
period, until Rosenzweig's death in 1929. In Europe, these years,
especially the late teens, were a time of intense reflection about language, its origin, nature, capacities, and limitations. Romantic theories of language—those of Humboldt, Hamann, and Herder—were
recovered and discussed, and also, especially during this period,
Kierkegaard was coming to be more widely read. [15] Fritz Mauthner's
influence on the early Wittgenstein and on Gustav Landauer is often
cited; also of significance was the work of Husserl, Frege, Dilthey,
and others on the social, psychological, and logical dimensions of

language and speech. *Lebensphilosophie* (Life Philosophy), Bergson, James, Brentano, and other figures and trends recommended a non-rationalist account of revelation, via some kind of intuition or imaginative experience. Even in such accounts, of course, language played a role. Language was associated with logic and rationality, on the one hand, but also with poetry and myth, on the other. To Buber, revelation was akin to the experience or act of poetic creativity; it was relational but not itself linguistic, although it issued in myth, poetry, and literary testimony. The limits of language are the limits of the world but not the limits of experience. Even Kant, on a certain reading, could be seen to agree with such a claim. To Rosenzweig, then, revelation was a direct encounter, akin to language in its capacity as a mechanism for mutual address and response, in its temporality, and in its character as a call to communication and action.

Language and Revelation: Benjamin and Scholem

In 1916, Walter Benjamin set down some early reflections on language entitled "On Language as Such and on the Language of Man."[16] In those years, Benjamin was interested in the very idea of experience, a theory of ideas, Kant, Plato, and language. His essay on language was written in Munich, where Benjamin in October 1915 had gone to live with his fiancée Grete Radt.[17] He had met Gershom Scholem in June 1915. It was a moment when the two students shared deep reservations about Buber, both about his reaction to the war and about the "cult of experience," which, lacking in moral depth, had formed around him. Scholem had been expelled from school for opposing the war, and he was repelled by Buber's Zionism, with its center in mystical experience. He read his own critique of the Jewish youth movement to Benjamin, who himself had broken with Gustav Wyneken and the youth movement over the valorization of the war. It was in this context that Benjamin and Scholem discussed language and its relation to extraordinary experiences, one product of which was Benjamin's essay. In December of 1916, Benjamin gave Scholem a copy of his paper.[18]

Scholem's early work on the Kabbalah, work that led to his dissertation on the *Sefer Ha-Bahir,* concerned the role of language in mystical thinking and activity.[19] Before we turn to Benjamin's essay, it is helpful to look at Scholem.

Scholem gives an excellent summary of his views about revelation and language in his famous later paper, "Revelation and Tradition as Religious Categories in Judaism."[20] Formulations and phrases used in this essay go back to the early conversations with Benjamin.[21] They recur in Scholem's correspondence with Benjamin in the 1930s about Kafka and Benjamin's essay about Kafka.

> In Judaism, tradition becomes the reflective impulse that intervenes between the absoluteness of the divine word—revelation—and its receiver. Tradition thus raises a question about the possibility of immediacy in man's relationship to the divine. . . . To put it another way: Can the divine word confront us without mediation? And, can it be fulfilled without mediation? Or, given the assumption of the Jewish tradition which we have formulated, does the divine word rather not require just such mediation by tradition in order to be apprehensible and therefore fulfillable? For rabbinic Judaism, the answer is in the affirmative. Every religious experience after revelation is a mediated one. It is the experience of the voice of God rather than the experience of God.[22]

In this later paper, Scholem asks how the authority and applicability of Judaism's original revelation can be and indeed *have* been preserved and conveyed, as historical circumstances change. His answer is that the Talmudic and then Kabbalistic notions of tradition have been the vehicle for this preservation. "Revelation needs commentary in order to be rightly understood and applied" (287; cf. 291). The original revelation "sets a task." Thereafter it must be understood and applied or, as Scholem often puts it, "apprehended and fulfilled." The question is: how can this pristine, remote, ultimately mysterious revelation, this truth, be received? And the answer is that in order to be received—apprehended and fulfilled—it must be mediated. "In Judaism, tradition becomes the reflective impulse that intervenes between the absoluteness of the divine word—revelation—and its receiver. . . . Can the divine word con-

front us without mediation? And can it be fulfilled without mediation? Or . . . does the divine word rather not require just such mediation by tradition in order to be apprehensible and therefore
fulfillable? For rabbinic Judaism, the answer is in the affirmative.
Every religious experience after revelation is a mediated one. It is
the experience of the voice of God rather than the experience of
God" (292).[23]

Scholem may be conceding too much to the original revelation
and its reception; even that encounter may have had to have been
mediated. But he surely concedes nothing to later "receptions." If
God—revelation—is to be in some way understood and if the divine
"task" is to be in some way fulfilled, then language must be the
bridge—text, commentary, tradition. Judaism involves a meaningful
way of life, an understanding of the world and humankind's role in
it, conduct performed in terms of that understanding and fulfillment
of the principles of that meaningful life. If so, Judaism is grounded
in a relationship with God, absolute and incomprehensible. How,
then, does an individual have access to that absolute divine will?
Through an act of divine disclosure and human reception. But if
the disclosure is an act of grace, what facilitates the reception and
makes it possible? It is the fact, Scholem claims, that all historical
receptions fix on the "voice of God" and not on God Himself. Revelation as tradition occurs in language; it is mediated.

It is Scholem's view that one of the great accomplishments of
the Kabbalists was to reflect on and articulate the "word of God,"
"the voice of God" (292 ff.). The essence of their conception was
that although in revelation God revealed only Himself, this self-
revelation was also a revelation of the name of God, out of which
the Torah is built up; "the whole Torah is nothing but the great
name of God" (294).[24] It is also infinitely interpretable and hence
fulfillable in a variety of ways. "There is no immediate, undialectical
application of the divine word. If there were, it would be destructive. . . . It is the tradition of the word of God . . . that permits its
application in history" (296). Hence, the scholar and commentator
makes the Torah and the revelation concrete at a moment of history;
this individual makes it relevant, receivable, fulfillable, and transmis-
sible, all at once. And although Scholem does not say so explicitly,

the act is not only receptive; it is also responsive and redemptive, insofar as it incorporates a fulfillment of the divinely grounded task in history. It is a hearing that is also a doing (296–97).

In the course of this account of revelation and tradition, Scholem refers to revelation as "absolute and meaning-giving but in itself meaningless" (296). He also says that "theologians have described the word of God as the 'absolutely concrete' . . . [which is] the simply unfulfillable—that which in no way can be put into practice" (296).[25] In other words, the divine disclosure orients human life, but in order to do so, it must take a form accessible to human experience. Scholem claims that the Kabbalists asked this Kantian question: what must revelation and tradition be like in order for man to grasp what is being disclosed, apply it to his situation, and fulfill it in his actions—put it into practice. And the Kabbalistic answer is: language, indeed levels of language from pure to everyday. This implies, as David Biale notes, that for Scholem, in contrast to Buber, Karl Barth, and his disciple Hans Joachim Schoeps, revelation is not immediate; the commentator, now the scholar, and not the ecstatic are the genuine religious practitioners.[26]

Benjamin, in his early essay on language, gives his own account of the nature of language and the role of language in man's relation to God. "God's creation is completed when things receive their names from man, from whom in name language alone speaks" (319).[27] At the same time, language is the vehicle of revelation (320–21); it is the only way the inexpressible can be grasped by man. Moreover, everyday language is the result of confusion, multiplicity, and dispersion, factors which make language part of daily discourse. Benjamin mythologizes language, creation, and the mundane world, imagining levels of language, from profane to pure, which frame creation on the one hand and redemption on the other. The role of language is to stretch out between God and man, God and nature, as a bridge. In short, what Benjamin conceptualizes, in a Platonic manner, is akin to what Scholem later takes to be a great achievement of the Kabbalists.[28]

The language of an entity is the medium in which its mental being is communicated. The uninterrupted flow of this communication runs through the whole of nature from the lowest forms of existence to man and from man to God. Man communicates himself to God through name, which he gives to nature and (in proper names) to his own kind, and to nature he gives names according to the communication that he receives from her, for the whole of nature, too, is imbued with a nameless, unspoken language, the residue of the creative word of God, which is preserved in man as the cognizing name and above man as the judgment suspended over him. The language of nature is comparable to a secret password that each sentry passes to the next in his own language, but the meaning of the password is the sentry's language itself. All higher language is a translation of those lower, until in ultimate clarity the word of God unfolds, which is the unity of this movement made up of language.[29]

Already in Benjamin's early essay, then, we find the view of revelation and language later employed by Scholem to explicate and clarify the Kabbalistic notions of revelation and redemption.[30] It is a view of language as the bridge between a pure revelation and a humanly interpreted reception of it.

From 1925 to 1929, when Rosenzweig died, he and Buber collaborated on their translation of the Bible into German, and Buber began what became a virtually life-long engagement with the Bible and its interpretation. Just prior to initiating their joint project, Rosenzweig had completed his translation of Halevi's poems and his notes on them. During the twenties, then, both Buber and Rosenzweig were involved in translation, specifically in translation of the Biblical text, interpretation of the literary tradition, and reflection about the relationship between revelation and the Jewish textual tradition. We have seen that for Scholem and Benjamin, whatever their differences, one motivation for their opposition to the Buber-Rosenzweig conception of revelation as pre-conceptual and immediate arose out of their convictions about commentaries, literary interpretation, and in general tradition. In Scholem's terms, the Word of God was in fact apprehended and fulfilled, but the "absolutely concrete" could be neither. Hence their conclusion, that revelation itself must be linguistic; immediate revelation could have no impact, no effect, and especially no literary development.

There are reasons to think that Scholem, in 1962, not only had the same view, then reinforced by his study of Kabbalistic texts, but that then too he opposed the view of revelation associated with Buber and Rosenzweig. Yet, the Buber-Rosenzweig collaboration on the Bible translation and Buber's continued work on the Bible intervened. Both in the translation project and in his Biblical interpretation, Buber suggested what he took to be the relationship between the Bible and the founding revelation of the Jewish people and that between the Bible and the possibility of revelation in the life of the contemporary Jewish reader. Here is an opportunity to see if his views, augmented by those of Rosenzweig, might withstand the criticism of Scholem and Benjamin. For them, the gap between a mysterious revelation and a literary tradition of text and commentary is unbridgeable; for Buber and Rosenzweig there is no such gap, given the Biblical testimony and our encounter with it. It is worth clarifying what their view was and what it says about revelation and language.

In a number of essays and notes, collected and published by Buber in 1935 as *Die Schrift und ihre Verdeutschung* (The Bible and Its Translation into German), he and Rosenzweig clarify what led to their joint effort to translate the Bible into German, how they proceeded, and their method of translation and its goals. In addition, Buber wrote several books and a host of articles on the Bible. We need not examine the details of the Buber-Rosenzweig method of translation and examples of it. But its general character and its goal are important. The method is oral, focusing on the vocal character of the text and the original auditory character of the narratives, poems, and more. Writing, in their view, may rescue a text, but it also hides or camouflages, as it reveals, the oral shape of the teaching. And since form and content interpenetrate, the oral character of the teaching is integral to what it is. Hence, the goal of the translation and then of interpretation of it is to reveal, expose, and understand the oral teaching that eventuated in the written text before us. The identification of cola and the use of the *Leitwort* to identify affinities of passages had as a goal the uncovering of the Bible's original message. That message, moreover, originated with the people's response to the address at Sinai and the teaching of that response, its transmission, and its reformulation, until it was canonized, as it were, by the author of the Biblical text. Both translation of the text, then, and subsequent interpretation of it aim to uncover that teaching and hence that response, in short what the original Sinaitic revelation meant to the people then confronted and called by God. How can a modern reader understand the covenantal relationship established then and how can such a reader appropriate that message for him or herself?[31]

For Buber and Rosenzweig, then, what is it that bridges the gap between the original, pristine moment of encounter and the people's initial response to it? What bridges the gap between the immediacy of the moment and the oral response, the exclamation of what that event meant for that people and its life with God? Nowhere, so far as I can see, does Buber clearly describe this transition. I-thou encounters and the encounter with the Eternal Thou are linguistic, speech-events of a pristine kind. And the human response to them very often is spoken as well. But to some, like Scholem and Benjamin, the original encounter is mysterious and incapable of being realized, of having an impact, an influence. Mediation is necessary at every level. Lack of it is a sign of mystification. Rosenzweig, in *The Star* (1921), connects the revelation with the response by means of the notion of love, a gracious love within the revelation that is imported into the human response to it. But still that leaves much unsaid.

The background to dealing with this question, I think, is Kantian. For Kant, human experience requires both sensory and conceptual input, both sensory intuitions and concepts of the understanding. In a sense, for Buber and Rosenzweig, revelation too requires both an element of passivity and one of activity or spontaneity; revelation begins with the divine presence in all its immediacy, but it is completed only when the human contributes its understanding, its shaping of the event into a teaching, a narrative, a principle, and finally an action. Hence, for Buber and Rosenzweig, there is nothing mysterious about how a brute encounter, pre-conceptual and intuitive, can issue in a written text and then a tradition of commentaries, reformulations, and conduct. This is no more myste-

rious than the Kantian account of experience itself, a synthesis required by our experience and understanding of the world. Revelation for them is the analogue of Kantian experience, the "absolutely
concrete" an analogue for the synthetic a priori.

Sensory intuition in Kant puts the brake to Kant's idealism; it is
insurance for realism. Similarly, in Buber and Rosenzweig, the Divine Presence is the hedge against relativism and anarchism. Scholem and Benjamin, who themselves have a problem with unbounded
interpretations and with objectivity, do not seem to accept this con-
straint. But one is hard put to imagine how the absolute equivocity
between human language and the Divine Word is a better safeguard.
Nor is it obvious how the positing of an original *Ursprache*, the
Divine Language, can save a written tradition, if the relation between the two is itself unconditionally equivocal. In a sense, the
same problem faces both: how does human response derive from an
original mystery? It does not matter in principle whether the original mystery is an unmediated encounter or a completely *sui generis*
language. In the Middle Ages, one prominent way to save such
equivocity was to install a doctrine of analogy, but while one finds
such a response in someone like Karl Barth, one does not find it
either in Buber or in Scholem.

We could, at this point, jump directly to Benjamin's reflections
on criticism, history, and the messianic. The redemptive role of literary criticism has already surfaced, and Benjamin's later thoughts
bring together revelation and redemption in a very special way. But
it will be helpful to interpolate a further step: the Benjamin-Scholem
conversation (correspondence) on Kafka. The difference between
the two regarding Kafka is centrally important; it concerns the presence or at least the prominence of God and revelation in this redemptive conception of critique.[32]

Scholem and Benjamin on Kafka

Scholem refers to Kafka in the tenth of his "Unhistorical Aphorisms on Kabbalah." [Biale's commentary is illuminating.[33]] The
text was published in 1958, long after his correspondence of the 1930s

(especially 1934) with Benjamin. But it recovers a genuine impulse in Scholem, for whom Kafka evoked a "heretical Kabbalah," the faith of a secular Jew committed to tradition.[34] Here was someone committed to the Law, to the tradition, but who also took revelation to be inherently inaccessible. Hence, the only way to disclose the hidden, to receive it, is to read the tradition adversely or, as Benjamin puts it, "against the grain."[35] The key to Scholem's reading of Kafka, as it was for his reading of the Kabbalistic tradition, was a two-fold commitment: both to the need for fulfillment, practice, and realizability and to the ground of the task, revelation and the hidden God. For Kafka, as it was for the Kabbalists, the challenge was to bridge the two, to fill in the gap, to make revelation receivable by making it linguistic or textual.[36] As Scholem himself points out, it is this mediated view of revelation that belies the theology of those like Buber and Schoeps.[37] Kafka is a deeply theological writer but not because he pessimistically portrays the human condition at a time of divine estrangement. Rather, he is theological because he realistically portrays the permanent human condition as one of life with the fragments of tradition, the only possible access to an inherently hidden truth.[38]

Scholem's differences with Benjamin over their readings of Kafka are reflected in their correspondence of 1934 and after. Benjamin had published his essay on Kafka in the *Judische Rundschau* in 1934; the correspondence ensued. This is the central passage from Benjamin's correspondence:

> Wisdom has sometimes been defined as the epic side of truth. Such a definition stamps wisdom as inherent in tradition; it is truth in its haggadic consistency.
>
> It is this consistency of truth that has been lost. Kafka was far from being the first to face this situation. Many had accommodated themselves to it, clinging to truth or whatever they happened to regard as truth and, with a more or less heavy heart, forgoing its transmissibility. Kafka's real genius was that he tried something entirely new: he sacrificed truth for the sake of clinging to its transmissibility, its haggadic element. Kafka's writings are by their nature parables. But it is their misery and their beauty that they had to become *more* than parables. They do not modestly lie at the feet of the doctrine, as

the Haggadah lies at the feet of the Halakah. Though apparently reduced to submission, they unexpectedly raise a mighty paw against it.

This is why, in regard to Kafka, we can no longer speak of wisdom. Only the products of decay remain. There are two: one is the rumor about the true things (a sort of theological whispered intelligence dealing with matters discredited and obsolete); the other . . . is folly. . . . Thus, as Kafka puts it, there is an infinite amount of hope, but not for us. This statement really contains Kafka's hope; it is the source of his radiant serenity.[39]

To Scholem, Kafka's writings are the work of a theological passion, even if they do not succeed.[40] They are an attempt to bridge the gap and enable a hidden revelation to become accessible. Benjamin differed with Scholem about Kafka's commitments, and their difference over Kafka may very well reflect an important difference between them as well.[41]

For Benjamin, Kafka must be understood against the background of theology, but he should not be interpreted in terms of a theological commitment.[42] Kafka is not committed to the truth, the absolute, or the divine. He is committed to life and to writing, to parables that portray and represent but precisely only themselves. This is what Benjamin says in his famous letter to Scholem of June 12, 1938, as he comments critically on Brod's biography. Benjamin claims there that for Kafka there is no doctrine, no knowledge, no truth. What is left is tradition, "the most indistinct sounds [that] reach the listener."[43] Gone is wisdom, tradition bound up with truth; what we have seen is the network of revelation with its mediated tradition. This is the contemporary situation, or at least Kafka's situation: a time when the divine and the human have been isolated one from the other, when, as Benjamin puts it, "truth in its aggadic consistency" has been lost. Benjamin contrasts Kafka to those who have dealt with this estrangement—Kierkegaard, Buber, Barth, Schoeps—by "clinging to truth or whatever they happened to regard as truth and . . . forgoing its transmissability." To these theologians—and there may be others too, poets, painters, and more—the divine truth is mysterious and the reception of it mysterious too. Like Scholem, Benjamin denigrates such an attempt; it is escapist, irrelevant, irrational, nostalgic, and anti-critical. But Benjamin credits Kafka with a wholly new alternative, unlike even a secular Kabbalah. "He sacrificed truth for the sake of clinging to its transmissability, its haggadic element. Kafka's writings are by their nature parables. But it is their misery and their beauty that they had to become *more* than parables."[44] What remains in these parables are the "products of decay," the rumor of the true things and folly. What Kafka sought was a structure of writing that did not answer theological questions but rendered these questions superfluous.[45]

Benjamin clarifies his differences with Scholem in 1934 (Letter 240, August 11, 1934; Letters, 4522–4554) and subsequently in his correspondence. To Scholem, on August 11, 1934, he writes that their starting-points differ: to Scholem it is the "nothingness of revelation"; to Benjamin it is "the small, nonsensical hope, as well as the creatures for whom this hope is intended and yet who on the other hand are also the creatures in which this absurdity is mirrored."[46] Scholem had charged Benjamin with eliminating theology from his reading of Kafka and with denial of the *existence* of Law.[47] Benjamin's response is to claim that he has not eliminated theology and Law but refocused on Kafka's treatment of life among humankind when theology has become problematic. Kafka's characters live "in the village at the foot of the hill on which the castle is built," and what Kafka's parables attempt to do is "to metamorphize life into Scripture."[48] For Benjamin, this "messianic task" is viewed from the writer's and the human perspective—how to transform profane life into the sacred. Whether or not the Law, God, or revelation exists—this is where "his work comes to a standstill" and "cannot be moved in any interpretive direction."[49] For Kafka, the task is to find the sacred in the mundane, a task at which he fails, according to Benjamin.[50]

In his account of Benjamin's affinity for Kafka,[51] David Stern has relied upon Hans Mayer's view, that Benjamin's understanding of theology in Kafka changed between 1934 and 1938. "According to Scholem, Kafka still believed in the possibility of revelation, but only as a kind of negative revelation, a revelation of nothingness in which all that could truly be revealed was the experience of revelation:. . . . For Benjamin, by contrast, the world of Kafka was one in which any kind of meaningful revelation had ceased to exist."[52] Hence, Kafka used parables to express the disintegration of tradition, Stern claims. But one must be very careful here. What has disintegrated is the status of texts and life *as* tradition, as disclosures of a hidden God, of revelation. Scholem treats Kafka as a neo-Kabbalist, giving new readings of revelation; Benjamin treats his art as a failed messianic attempt to recover the divine in the profane. The crucial shift here is not from theology to its denial but rather from conceptualizing Kafka within the category of revelation to conceptualizing him within the category of redemption and a redemption grounded in the literary creativity of the writer and reader.

Robert Alter claims that regarding Kafka, the issue between Scholem and Benjamin in their correspondence of 1934–1938 is between "an absent and an unintelligible revelation."[53] He is absolutely correct. Alter goes on to make the useful point that for Scholem revelation figured in an understanding of tradition—"written words, commentaries and supra-commentaries"—while Benjamin's thinking about revelation was focused on the concept of aura, the temporal dimension of which is memory and the associations in the mind that cluster and cloud around the object of perception.[54] Alter quotes Scholem's letter of July 17, 1934, where Scholem takes the crucial difference between Benjamin and himself to be whether the revelation in Kafka is absent or unfulfillable.[55] Benjamin could see no significance in the distinction; he says as much in his letter of August 11, 1934: "Whether the pupils have lost [the Scripture] or whether they are unable to decipher it comes down to the same thing, because, without the key that belongs to it, the Scripture is not Scripture, but life. Life as it is lived in the village at the foot of the hill on which the castle is built."[56] Scholem could see a difference, as he spells out on September 20, 1934: revelation exists but in itself does not mean anything—this is what is "the nothingness of revelation."[57] Alter ties this notion of "nothingness" to Scholem's statement, "the absolutely concrete can never be fulfilled at all," which Scholem had used in his critique of Schoeps in 1932 and would again repeat in his famous Eranos lecture in 1962. This is the challenge not only for Kabbalistic theology but also for all legitimate theology and hence for all human existence.[58] And for Scholem this challenge is portrayed both in the Kabbalistic tradition and in Kafka's parables.

Hence, Scholem's point about Kafka is a general point about the human condition: "the world in which we find ourselves has an ultimate, though also ultimately inscrutable, semantic power." In the end, for Scholem, "human consciousness" and "ultimate being" are bound to one another.[59] For Benjamin, on the other hand, Kafka wrote not about life in a world with such a "distant" revelation; what "caught his eye was Kafka's brilliant dramatization of man's alienation from both self and fellow man."[60] Man's alienation, too, from that ultimate being, from revelation, from God.

To clarify how Scholem and Benjamin differ concerning Kafka, it is helpful to compare their views of Kafka with Buber's, best expressed in his book of 1951, *Two Types of Faith*. Buber reads Kafka's *The Trial* and *The Castle* as similes of the contemporary situation. They portray man estranged from God, hopeless in his dealings with his own soul and with the world, his life meaningless and absurd. At one point, Buber says that Kafka's world is one in which God hides His face, a term he uses for a time of evil, of the "eclipse of God."

Buber's account stands somewhere between Scholem's and Benjamin's. Unlike both, Buber sees Kafka's world as distinctive, unusual, a time of deep historical estrangement. For Scholem and for Benjamin, in contrast, Kafka portrays the human condition in general, in all its normality, so to speak. For Scholem, however, the human task is to try to grasp, by means of commentary, interpretation, and tradition, the hidden meaning of the revelation that directs all things. Benjamin and Buber differ. For them, Kafka depicts the world and human life when that revelation either does not exist or is too alienated to matter.

Alter's interpretation, then, is very helpful and largely correct. There is a sense in which revelation—truth, wisdom, Torah—is the central difference between Scholem and Benjamin regarding Kafka and perhaps personally as well. Furthermore, that difference marks a shift in Benjamin's thinking from an emphasis on revelation to one on redemption.

This shift puts us in a position to appreciate Benjamin's late reflections on literary criticism and history. If there is a shift from 1934 to 1938 in Benjamin's thinking about Kafka, in part it is about what Kafka is doing or attempting to do, with his parables, stories, and novels. Resignation and description give way to redemptive energy and failure. Benjamin is convinced throughout these years that Kafka has no conviction about the divine and the possibility of revelation. Hence, unlike Scholem, Benjamin does not read Kafka as a quasi-Kabbalist, constructing or continuing the tradition that mediates between that revelation and its apprehension and fulfillment. What theology there is in Kafka all resides at the level of hope or at least aspiration or desire. In Kafka's world, there is no revelation and no Law, but there is a desire to find one or the other, to use the literary strategies of tradition to make life into a route to the divine. Kafka, like Rosenzweig, cultivates an openness whereby even mundane, prosaic acts can becomes venues for human encounter with the Absolute. They *can be*, although, in Benjamin's judgement, they do not. They fail.

Benjamin, History, and Redemptive Critique

There are a host of questions raised by the notion of redemption; Benjamin addresses some of them early on in his "Theologico-Political Fragment," probably written in 1920–1921.[61] The primary theme of these notes, which may have been preparatory to a review of Ernst Bloch's *Geist der Utopie* (1918), is the relation between history or the political, on the one hand, and redemption or the messianic, on the other. Benjamin begins the fragment with an affirmation that hides a denial: "Only the Messiah himself consummates all history. . . . " The implication is that human effort *does not* perfect history. Hence, as Benjamin goes on, "the Kingdom of God is not the *telos* of the historical dynamic. . . . it is not the goal, but the end."[62] History is the domain of human action, of the political; the

messianic is the domain of a perfect resolution that is neither political nor grounded in human agency. Benjamin cites this teaching,
of the radical discontinuity between the political and the theocratic,
as the central contribution of Ernst Bloch's *Geist der Utopie,* and
in the remainder of the fragment goes on to elaborate and appropriate it. He asks, how then are the historical-political and the
theological-messianic related? This is "one of the essential teachings
of the philosophy of history," a "mystical conception of history."[63]
The relation, he says, is one of "assistance": the order of the profane
(history, the political, human agency) assists the coming of the messianic kingdom. Benjamin provides an image: the messianic intensity and human, profane acts are two arrows that intersect from different directions (opposite?), the one reacting to the other. History
is the domain of downfall, misfortune, and destruction; it is the
domain of nature, desire, competition, conflict, and "nihilism," and
it is "Messianic by reason of its eternal and total passing away."[64]
World politics, as he puts it, strives for such passing away, to which
the Messiah responds with redemptive intensity.

In this trenchant text, to summarize, Benjamin makes these
points: that history and the redemptive are discontinuous, that history is the domain of politics and nature, that history is a heap of
ruins, that the agency of the redemptive is the Messiah, and that
human agency "assists" but does not bring about redemption. By
the time he had written his letter to Scholem about Kafka and Brod's
biography in 1938, Benjamin had certainly changed his mind about
some features of this configuration. History is still ruins, but the
literary critic and the writer have replaced the Messiah as the agency
of redemption. Indeed, their activity constitutes the straight gate
through which the Messiah enters the world.

Moreover, redemption can occur only when a bridge is created
between the present and the past, each illuminating the other. The
past "assists" redemption not only by its destructive character but
also by the illumination that hides beneath its surface, an illumination to be released through the special achievement of literary, historical critique and by the creation of what he calls crystallizations
or configurations, monads, and "dialectical images."

To observe these changes, we must turn to Benjamin's justly famous theses on the concept of history, which he wrote in the final months of his life in 1940 as the theoretical presuppositions that supported his unfinished Arcades Project.[65] As commentators have often noted, these are rich aphorisms. They exhibit the intersection of Benjamin's messianism and his historical materialism, both of which he shaped in extraordinarily idiosyncratic ways. They also reflect his appropriation of surrealist motifs. We are especially interested in Benjamin's understanding of the redemptive agency of critique and the relation between redemption and history, what he calls "a secret agreement between past generations and the present one."[66] Among the central passages from Benjamin's "Theses" are these:

> Thinking involves not only the flow of thoughts, but their arrest as well. Where thinking suddenly stops in a configuration pregnant with tensions, it gives that configuration a shock, by which it crystallizes into a monad. A historical materialist approaches a historical subject only where he encounters it as a monad. In this structure he recognizes the sign of a messianic cessation of happening, or, put differently, a revolutionary chance in the fight for the oppressed past.[67]

> Historicism contents itself with establishing a causal connection between various moments in history. But no fact that is a cause is for that very reason historical. It became historical posthumously, as it were, through events that may be separated from it by thousands of years. A historian who takes this as his point of departure stops telling the sequence of events like the beads of a rosary. Instead, he grasps the constellation which his own era formed with a definite earlier one. Thus he establishes a conception of the present as the "time of the now" which is shot through with chips of messianic time.[68]

Throughout the theses, Benjamin makes the point again and again that the past is a function of the present. And the present is potentially messianic; it can be redemptive. If it is, then the past is properly grasped and the present somehow transformed. First we must ask about the present.

To historians, the present can be a problem, for the present embodies the historian's prejudices and biases, and those, some argue, distort the historian's judgments about the past, the use of evidence, selectivity, narrative, and more.[69] On the other hand, as Nietzsche claimed, history is significant only when it is relevant to the present; otherwise, it is mere antiquarianism.[70] The present incorporates the needs, the interests, and the current urgencies that point to the past and make certain events, people, and actions illuminating and valuable. In a sense, only in terms of the present and its demands does the past take shape. The historical perspective is unavoidable; so-called detached historiography is one stance among many. Textual and non-textual evidence exists in the present; it has a past dimension, a vector. But with respect to which evidence to focus on and how to interpret it, these things depend upon *other* features of the present—the historian's situation, its problems, needs, and character. Over time, events deposit residue that continues to exist; at every present moment this residue is what remains; it is evidence to be examined and interpreted. All of this—residue, problems, historian, and so forth—is the present. From one point of view, the past is unavoidably relative to this present; from another, the past only exists in the present, as a present recollection of what no longer exists.

Benjamin's views are along these lines: "There is a secret agreement between past generations and the present one. Our coming was expected on earth. Like every generation that preceded us, we have been endowed with a *weak* Messianic power. . . . "[71] The past always looks forward to a particular future that is redemptive and culminating. But that future is any particular present, which has the capacity to be redemptive. When it succeeds, it becomes the end of the historical story, what the past was pointing to. This is what Benjamin means when he says that "only a redeemed mankind receives the fullness of the past."[72] Moreover, to him the urgency of the present is the class struggle, the fight for food and clothing, for justice, that enables "courage, humor, cunning, and fortitude."[73] Therefore, every present is a potential vestibule to a redeemed past, one that is won back from the oppression of the ruling class. One of the results of the victories of the ruling class, the enemy, is the creation of cultural objects; another is the dominant account of the past itself, for "*even the dead* will not be safe from the enemy if he wins."[74] Since the victors have been those who rule and oppress, Benjamin can say that "there is no document of civilization which is not at the same time a document of barbarism." This is why one cannot read texts as they present themselves or take cultural artifacts at face value. Rather, the task of the genuine historian, the literary and cultural critic, is "to brush history against the grain," to interpret existing evidence contrary to apparent meaning and significance, to disclose what it hides about oppression, injustice, and suffering.[75]

Benjamin identifies and opposes three views of the past—historicism, liberalism, and what might be called imperialism. Historicism is the view that there is one true past, spread out as a "chain of events" or a "sequence of events [arranged] like the beads of a rosary," and that the historian's job is to "establish a causal connection" between them or to recognize "the way it really was."[76] For Benjamin, on the contrary, there exists in every present a vast residue from the past, in the form of cultural relics and literary objects that are evidence for a host of pasts, depending upon how those relics and texts are understood.

Secondly, historical imperialism accepts the stories of the past, established and traditional historical narratives, as the ruling class tells them. Rulers finance culture, sponsor historical writing, patronize the arts; moreover, many others affiliate with their perspective insofar as their success spells the success of the literate, the articulate, and the elite. Hence, architecture, painting, books—all seem to tell certain stories. But Benjamin rejects them and in fact wants all genuine historical thinking to do so as well. Such stories are really tales of oppression that hide rather than expose suffering and its causes.

Finally, in his day Benjamin takes the current state of emergency to be the rise and dominance of fascism. The particular historical narrative to be rejected is that of Enlightenment liberalism, capitalism, the Social Democrats, and the associated conception of progress.[77] The latter developed one picture, a universal history of mankind in which human beings achieve greater and greater perfectibility. Such a view not only relies on a falsely optimistic view of human nature; it also adheres to a false view of continuous, homogeneous time.

Benjamin, then, rejects historicism, imperialism, and Enlightenment liberalism. What he calls "historical materialism" is his favored alternative. It recognizes oppression, injustice, and the present stage of emergency; it appreciates that there are many pasts, each tied to different presents; it is redemptive or messianic; and it has a correct understanding of time.[78]

What is the historical materialist view of time? And how does the present become redemptive? For Benjamin and the historical materialist, as he sees him, time is made up of discrete episodes, units of experience, action, and thinking. Time starts with the present, what he calls the "now time" [*Jetztzeit*]; when it incorporates a grasp of the past via thinking about an artifact, text, or cultural object, then the present and the past cohere in an image, and the present has thereby a historical dimension.[79] Time, then, is an experiential episode that incorporates reference to one or more pasts or futures. Time past is a changing array of past episodes, events, actions, and so forth referred to within one or more presents. All time is oriented around individual experience, thinking, and insight.

Perhaps the most exciting features of the aphorisms are Benjamin's suggestive comments on historical thinking as redemptive or messianic, what actualizes the "weak Messianic power" of any given present instant. The past is present as texts, artifacts, or residue, what Benjamin calls ruins or debris. When properly interpreted, from the vantage point of a present sensitive to the contemporary "state of emergency," the past is present as an image. "The past can be seized only as an image which flashes up at the instant when it can be recognized," Benjamin says. He continues, "To articulate the past historically does not mean to recognize it 'the way it really was' (Ranke). It means to seize hold of a memory as it flashes up at a moment of danger. . . . The danger affects both the content of the tradition and its receivers. The same threat hangs over both: that of becoming a tool of the ruling classes."[80] The critical historian, let us call him or her, grasps the danger, that is, he or she understands the contemporary situation as one of danger, of injustice, suffering, and oppression. Relics of the past call forth memories of past dangers akin to the present one. The mind "seizes" the two, past and present, in an image that sheds light on both. When the critical historian has this insight, the moment is in the process of realizing its redemptive potential, for our understanding of the past and the present are being liberated, redeemed from conformity to oppressive readings. When this occurs, the past, Benjamin says, is being "blasted out of the continuum of history." A revolution is beginning, a dialectical tiger's leap into the past.[81] At this moment, "time stands still and has come to a stop"; old, conventional history is interrupted. An episode of thought occurs which "arrests" the flow of conventional thoughts in a single image.[82] Benjamin describes the arrest this way: thinking stops in a tense configuration, which the thinking then "shocks," crystallizing it into a monad. The critic, a historical materialist, recognizes in this monad a "Messianic" halting of history and thereby "blasts" a "specific" era, now revealed as one of domination, out of the story of the victors, exposing in this Messianic moment the way that the linear narrative camouflages and hides the oppression of the victims.[83] The present is a "now time" "which is shot through with chips of Messianic time." And since this cognitive constellation, this image, can be grasped or seized at any moment, "every second of time [is] the strait gate through which the Messiah might enter."[84]

Benjamin's language in these aphorisms blends together terms from the Kabbalah and Jewish tradition, Marxism, and surrealism. What he describes is an alternative, revolutionary form of historical understanding. Its goal is to disclose the hidden meaning of past events for present experience, when the emergencies of the present are recognized. The cognitive mode is an image, the grasping or seizing of an image in thought. He also calls it a crystallization or a configuration or monad that is "pregnant with tension." Themes, notions, images, and principles from the past and the present are brought together, juxtaposed as in a montage, and the result is an interplay of illumination, reaction, and more. The language that Benjamin uses here is doubtless drawn from surrealism, the method of collage and literary montage. It calls for the juxtaposition of dis-

parate fragments for the purposes of mutual interaction, and a col-
lision of images.[85]

Critical here is the agency for this historical, redemptive act. It is
the politically, morally attuned historian—the literary critic and in-
terpreter of cultural relics. If every instant has revolutionary and
messianic potential, it is the critic who releases it. Reading the tradition is a redemptive act. There is no mention of the divine here,
no assumption that the agency of redemption is the Messiah. This
is a humanistic messianism. Human beings have the capacity to transcend linear history, the conventional continuum, and then to reen-
ter or interrupt it, to be revolutionary. Every such act changes the
present and the past.

Redemption is pluralistic. History or the past is redeemed from
the oppression of the victorious, the ruling classes. The evidence—
relics, texts, artifacts—is redeemed from layers of conformity and
from the clutches of the dominant narrative. The present is redeemed from the dangers and the suffering that beset it. Hence, in
Benjamin's day, contemporary life is redeemed from fascism, injustice, and oppression, from what Arendt would call "total domination" and violence.

Benjamin's early thoughts about language lead indirectly, then,
to his later thoughts about history, messianism, and redemption. In
his early essay, language and all expressions of the human spirit—
cultural artifacts—must be examined and understood in order to
uncover the pure, divine language. In his late reflections, Benjamin
saw this critical enterprise not as securing divine revelation but
rather as a way of redeeming the past and the present, of bringing
about the Kingdom of God. Literary criticism becomes a redemptive act.

There is a connection, then, between Benjamin's and Scholem's
conception of revelation and language, on the one hand, and Benjamin's thoughts about historical materialism, history, and messianism, on the other. Scholem argued that revelation had to take the
form of language to be apprehensible and fulfillable. Putting it in
these terms, Benjamin shows how, through the examination of language, that fulfillment occurs. They differ, however, over the possi-

bility of revelation and the role of God. Benjamin, in 1920–1921, seems to have assumed that only the Messiah—and God—can consummate history; this is no longer his view in 1938–1940. By then, Benjamin was convinced that any moment has a messianic potential but that the critical historian alone can realize the potential by "seizing hold of a memory as it flashes up at a moment of danger."

From Revelation to Redemption Today

It is not surprising that in postwar America, Buber and Rosenzweig were recovered as sources for the favored response to naturalism and rationalism. American Jewish life was in a process of liberation; it was increasingly affluent, materialistic, assimilated, and driven by social aspirations. Postwar Jewish theology in America was then dominated by a kind of popularized rationalism in the spirit of Hermann Cohen, by a naturalism grounded in Mordecai Kaplan's prewar account of a reconstruction of Judaism on the basis of modern social sciences, and by a new theological existentialism, imported from the continent. The centerpiece of the latter was the Buber-Rosenzweig conception of revelation and faith. In response to rampant assimilation and secularism, it was an influential view through the sixties and into the period of post-Holocaust Jewish thought. Its central goal was to recover the centrality of faith and God for Judaism in the modern world. Perhaps the best representative of postwar Jewish existentialism is Emil Fackenheim, the foremost neo-Buberian of the period, whose commitment to the same view of revelation and faith is manifest throughout his essays of the fifties and sixties, in *God's Presence in History* in 1970, in *Encounters between Judaism and Modern Philosophy* in 1972, and then in *To Mend the World* in 1983 and continually to this day.

But in the seventies and eighties, other trends emerged in American Jewish thought. One was a revised naturalism, where the experience of the divine in prayer and other spiritual contexts is conceived in psychological terms. Another has been a renewed interest in Maimonides and medieval rationalism, a movement that amounts to a revised natural theology. Finally, and perhaps most influentially, there has been a turn to textual study and to the interpretation of Bible, midrash, commentaries, kabbalistic texts, and much else within the Jewish tradition. For some this textual study is a vehicle for the recovery of the pristine Torah and hence of an original relationship with the divine, and for these something like the Scholem view of traditional commentaries might very well support their textual study. For others, however, textual study carries with it no such goal. Rather than the means for a return to the divine, it actually is treated as an end in itself or, possibly more accurately, it becomes the way to understand more profoundly our own day and its crises and urgencies. But there is no hope, for such readers, that the study of Bible, midrash, and commentaries will draw one closer to God; interpretation becomes not the bridge to the religious life but its surrogate through and through. In a sense, in the spirit of Benjamin's reading of Kafka, it is carried out while the divine and a commitment to transcendence are "bracketed."

These conceptions of revelation and redemption are in part a response to views like those of Buber and Rosenzweig, Schoeps and Barth. It is not clear, however, that they are successful responses. Why must revelation take the form of language? If Scholem is right, only then can revelation be apprehensible and fulfillable. But Scholem, in his account of the Kabbalistic theory of the name of God and of Torah, must accept a wholly speculative cosmological picture for which there is no evidence and only the thinnest of arguments. According to Scholem and Benjamin, Buber must accept the paradox of a divine-human encounter in which the absolute and conditioned participate and which both survive. But Scholem's Kabbalists and Benjamin, in his early essay on language, must simply posit both the distinctness and the continuity of divine and human language. Once these are set down as absolutely equivocal, the paradox of communication between the finite or conditioned and the infinite or absolute is simply replicated at the level of language.[86] The human apprehension of the divine task and its fulfillment are made possible, the argument goes, only if the revelation itself is linguistic. Only then can the interpretive, commentative tradition occur as grounded in an original text, the Torah and the divine name. But, one might object, if the language of the Torah and the divine name, the original language, are both pure and absolutely secret and the tradition is public, multiple, and prosaic, it is still a mystery how that communication can take place. Is it more than a pious hope that human interpretation of historically situated language can uncover the secrets of the pure, absolute language of God?

Perhaps Benjamin's later thought is more attractive, with its modesty about revelation and realism about redemption. His critique of conventional historiography has much to recommend it. Historical narratives *do* reflect the biases of those who wrote them, those who authorized them, and hence those who rule, the patrons of memory. If one's contemporary sense of society, its problems and dangers, and of the way that institutions and public portrayal hide those dangers are accurate, then one has every reason to suspect the surface meaning of cultural artifacts and historical accounts. Benjamin is certainly right about this kind of camouflage and suppression; he is also right that all history and cultural memory are a function of present concerns and interests. But Benjamin's response to this situation is the notion of a constellation or crystallization that is grasped by the mind and that brings together the past and the present in an image of mutual illumination, what he calls a "profane illumination." This conception, however, is no more determinate, even in form, than is the response to the immediacy of the divine-human encounter in Buber and others. The latter may be relative and non-rational, but surely Benjamin's dialectical images, the objects of an intuitive grasp, are no more rational or objectively structured. What Benjamin's account does include essentially is the presence in the image of both understandings of the past and of the present. It is through and through a way of integrating into one act of understanding evidence from the past, a re-reading of that evidence, and hence a subversive or suspicious reading of the past in terms of its relevance for the present and its clarification. These features are important and essentially historical. In the views of Buber and others, the role of the past is less primary and more contingent. In fact, the past might be ignored altogether. There is no way that for Benjamin this can be done.

In his discussion of "dialectical images," John McCole raises the question of objectivity.[87] McCole does not believe that Benjamin lapsed into "historical relativism." Benjamin is committed to a "true image of the past" and of the present. These arise out of "dialectical images" that realize "reciprocal illumination." "However decidedly he took leave of the idea of timeless truth, he did not surrender the idea of objectivity along with it."[88] I think that McCole is right, but how does Benjamin save this objectivity? Benjamin is committed to the partiality of any view of the truth; one's grasp of the present is always limited and only so much of the past is available to any present thinker. As McCole hints, however, from the messianic point of view, all is visible and clear. Is this concept compatible with Benjamin's rejection of revelation? I think that it is. What Benjamin rules out is our certainty about revelation; we must live as if there is no revelation. Whether it does not exist or whether it is simply utterly mysterious is irrelevant. Still, there can be true and false understandings of past and present; there is traditional distortion as well as clarity and illumination. Empirical conditions such as suffering, injustice, and oppression are indications of falsity and distortion. As one discloses the truth of one past episode after another, more will cohere, of past and present, until, when the Messiah comes, all will be clear. In short, Benjamin is not secular through and through; he does not deny absolutely and utterly the existence of revelation and the divine. What he denies is its historical impact, its effect. Life goes on, traditions take shape, redemption occurs— whether or not revelation does not exist or is beyond human accessibility. As Kafka says—there is hope, but not for us.[89]

Or is there? If we turn once more to the impact of the Holocaust, we find Emil Fackenheim. While he conceives of revelation as a direct encounter between the divine and the human, Fackenheim takes the religious responsibility of contemporary Jews, in the shadow of catastrophe, to be this: to recover the texts, rituals, and fullness of traditional Jewish life, in part as an obligation to keep Judaism and the Jewish people alive and in part as an obligation to keep open the possibility of reestablishing the divine-human relationship in a world where it has been severely challenged and where it has eroded. In short, for Fackenheim, revelation today, like redemption, can be an aspiration and, at least for some, a hope. Both divine Presence and human receptivity are uncertain, fraught with doubt, and at best the objects of hope. Many find even this much openness and receptivity to be too much to seek and too much to hope for. Indeed, even Fackenheim now wonders whether his conviction, argued in the central chapter of *To Mend the World,* that resistance and recovery are possible as well as necessary is not too optimistic or at least too facile a dismissal of a foreboding alternative view, that the *Musselmanner*—the living dead who populated the death camps—is the paradigm of a genuine response to Auschwitz. If that were true, then there is no hope; there is nothing but submission, degradation, and indeed death.

In Fackenheim, then, as in Rosenzweig and in Scholem, Jewish life is grounded in obligation and is directed to the texts, commentaries, rituals, and "mending of the world" that were in the past and once more in our day are the substance of Jewish existence. In all three, albeit differently, all that Jews have thought and done can still be the bridge between where today's Jew stands and the truth that he or she seeks to reach. Some will find the notion of revelation that underscores the views of Rosenzweig and Fackenheim appealing. Others will be attracted to Buber's view, similar to Rosenzweig's. Like Benjamin's conception, Buber's notion of revelation merges with redemptive responsibility, although with greater optimism. There are those, moreover, for whom revelation seems altogether incoherent and others for whom language must occur as the vehicle for making revelation "understandable and fulfillable." We live in a time of great uncertainty about what the divine and our relationship to it might be. It may not be clear whether ongoing revelation and our experience of God should be conceived in terms of reason, language, or a direct dialectical encounter. For now, no theory of revelation may seem compelling.

But theory is one thing; life another. We may find it difficult to make clear what revelation means to us and whether we can commit ourselves to one view of it. But the mandate to live as Jews remains. Once again, Fackenheim here is a person of vision and sensitivity.

In the shadow of the Holocaust, in a world of shifting sensibilities and moral uncertainty, we do not have the luxury to pause until a satisfying theory arrives, one compelling to all and bearing with it sufficient unanimity. Rather, we can sense a mandate to bring Judaism to life, even without confidence about revelation and its role. What views like those of Buber, Rosenzweig, Scholem, Benjamin, and Kafka all share is the investment in a life of texts, rituals, and a life of "hesitant openness." Ours is a situation of risk and danger and hence is suited to no more certainty than this, to face the future with both anticipation and concern and yet with the hope that the Jewish people will survive. For some, that is the limit of their hope; for others, the hope is greater still, to survive until the day when our relationship with "our cruel and merciful God" is once again secure. Life cannot and should not wait for reconciliation or clarification; with or without a theory of revelation, it must be lived, and what all these thinkers share is that commitment—a life lived with the texts, practices, artifacts, and traditions of the past.

3

MESSIANISM AND POLITICS

Incremental Redemption

Redemption and Politics: Their Interrelation

A hundred years ago, at the turn of the century, modern Zionism was in the midst of its first decade, and even then, it was clear to many that Zionism was a messianic movement, a movement deeply implicated in Judaism's historical destiny, its goals, and its hopes. The conflicts between Theodore Herzl and Ahad Ha-Am may not have been couched in messianic or redemptive language, but the Zionist aspirations of others as diverse as Leon Pinsker, Moses Hess, and Rav Kook were, as were too the doubts and demurrals of religious leaders who saw such political activity as a symptom of hubris. Indeed, such messianic language is still with us today; many share it, many oppose it, and while those on the political and religious right are most often associated with messianism, their ways of combining messianic language and Zionism are neither uniform nor exclusive. There are and have been liberal and socialist Zionists as well as eschatological ones.

Throughout the century, from that time to our own, the issue of how Jewish ideals and goals should register in political action and social engagement has been a persistent conundrum, and the issue is far broader than the ways in which Zionism and messianism intersect or repel each other. Human self-reliance has waxed and waned according to the fluctuations in our confidence in God and our skepticism about human capabilities. Doubts about human self-confidence, inflicted by World War I, have only been underscored, if not magnified, in the shadow of the Nazi horrors. What remains of liberal ideals and aspirations, our commitments to justice, dignity, and freedom from oppression and domination, has been seriously eroded by our recognition of the atrocities that humankind is fully capable of performing. Like our predecessors a century ago, we too wonder how utopian hopes are related to political realities, how eternity is related to time.

From one point of view, this problem about messianism or redemption, on the one hand, and politics, on the other, is a variation on the more general problem about the nature of history and the relationship between history and our conception of an ideal or utopian condition. One way of formulating the problem is to ask whether this ideal and history are continuous or whether, alternatively, history must come to an end or experience a radical disruption before the ideal condition, the result of some transcendent or vertical incursion, is established. Whether history is seen as linear and progressive or episodic, we can legitimately wonder whether the ideal condition is a continuation or development of it or the outcome of an interruption in it. One might even imagine this ideal condition, the kingdom of God or the *y'mot ha-mashiah* (days of the Messiah), as both of these, the continuation of one type of history and political action and the ultimate culmination of another non-linear, even circular historical life; this is one way, I believe, of understanding what Franz Rosenzweig calls his "messianic theory of knowledge" and his two-fold conception of the covenant and of Jewish and Christian history. But even such a synthesis is built on a distinction between a redemption that perfects and one that replaces historical experience.

From another point of view, this problem is about the relevance of social, political, and moral action to our conceptions of the messianic ideal. In what way, if any, does human action *contribute* to the realization of ideal human community? Liberals, socialists, and Marxists have regularly shared the conviction that it *does* contribute; indeed, for many it is hard to conceive of the realization of an ideal society without human effort in its behalf. Religious thinkers, of course, have often had less confidence in human capacity; hence they have regularly struggled to find a way of reconciling the ultimate need for divine redemptive intervention and the simultaneous desirability of human participation in social, political, and moral action. Rabbinic texts speak of both situations, of the coming of the Messiah when the world is both as evil and sinful as it could be and as perfect as human effort alone can make it; of the injunction to a life of waiting and prayer and a life of action to plant, build, and repair. In our own day, Jews at home in the modern secular world, if they hold messianic views at all, tend toward the Enlightenment view that progress toward an ideal human society is a human responsibility that is both worthy of our pursuit and ultimately realizable. But there are others, among them Orthodox Jews of various kinds, whose beliefs about redemption are wholly theocentric; redemption is God's alone.

What, however, of the relationship between the messianic ideal and political action in the other direction, from the redemptive point of view? Here, too, the connection is not so secure, even today in our highly secular culture. If we ask about *the relevance of the messianic to the political,* the problem is as challenging to secular moral and political thought as it is to the religious thinker. In recent years, for example, influential political theorists like John Rawls and Bruce Ackerman have argued for a conception of the liberal republic in which conceptions of the good life, held by individuals and associated with groups including religious communities, conceptions that include some redemptive or messianic ideal, are treated as *irrelevant* to political life.[1] Indeed, these theorists argue vigorously for the political neutrality of such thick theories of the good, as Rawls calls them; they cannot be allowed to influence the basic structures of liberal society, its principles of justice and the laws and policies that follow from them. If, therefore, the liberal, just society in fact were to contribute to the realization of some specific messianic conception, the kingdom of God as some particular group conceives it, that would be an accident. Liberal society is not a stage on the way to the realization of such an ideal; with respect to such conceptions, it may itself be an accommodation, a *modus vivendi,* a

compromise and the best we can hope for in the interim situation
that is history. In short, according to some liberal theorists, politics
is religiously and metaphysically neutral; religion and political life
are radically detached from each other and with this detachment
comes the associated detachment of the messianic from the political.

This separation of the religious and the political is deeply embedded in the Christian tradition. It is present in Luther. Moreover,
it is even found, although in a more complicated way, in Hobbes's
Erastianism in his important work *Leviathan*. A careful reading of
that work's third part, with its treatment of Scripture and the Christian commonwealth, recommends a distinction between sacred and
profane history and the placing of Hobbes's own political theory
solely within the latter. From this vantage point, Hobbes's account
of the state of nature and the social contract that establishes the
commonwealth and its government may themselves be a kind of
modus vivendi, an accommodation to the normal existence of human
beings in the natural world, to their needs, desires, and drives, especially the drive for self-preservation. On this account, as Hobbes
sees it, most people in the "state of nature" do not come to acknowledge the laws of nature as "divine commands." One cannot assume
universal adherence to Christian faith. Rather, the laws of nature
are, as it were, "theorems of reason," norms that all natural human
beings, given their constitution and that of their neighbors, recognize as desirable, if universalized within the society as a whole. As
long as Christianity and Christian faith are not universal, we live in
profane time or profane history, and the only way to maximize our
lives and well-being is through the kind of rational agreement that
yields a unity of us all in a social group and then a government with
the power and authority to prevent us from threatening and harm-
ing each other. Once Christian faith is universal, however, or if it
were to become so, then such a social and political structure would
be unnecessary. Eschatology is not the goal of politics but rather its
hope and, in the end, its replacement. Nor does politics contribute
to our messianic goals. For that, what is required is faith and a special kind of submission to God, the real God and not the "man-
made" God that is Hobbes's Leviathan.[2] Hobbes was a Christian

philosopher, I would contend, at least of a certain sort. But the same issues arise, albeit in different forms, for Jewish thinkers.

In the case of Moses Mendelssohn, for example, politics and religion share a common goal, the perfection of moral virtue in each individual. Religions, Judaism among them, seek to facilitate that goal through education and exhortation; civil society does so through justice, benevolence, and law. When individuals, in the state of nature, choose to establish a civil society with its sovereign and agencies, they choose to act based on personal desires, needs, knowledge, and moral principles. They want to cultivate moral virtue and want others to do so as well. Individuals by nature are aware of the duties they owe and the rights they possess; they want to perform those duties and to protect those rights, individually and collectively. Government is a set of institutions and laws implemented to facilitate this process. Mendelssohn tells this story in Part One of *Jerusalem,* as part of his understanding of the basic continuity among Judaism, liberal politics, and the goal of moral perfection, his redemptive ideal. For Mendelssohn, then, unlike Hobbes and several of our contemporaries, conceptions of the good, redemptive ideals, do shape political institutions and political conduct.

Mendelssohn is no anomaly. Some notion of messianism, of the directedness of history, of a social and communal ideal that we associate with God's purposes for humankind—all of this is too deeply embedded in the Jewish tradition for us to ignore the complexity of these issues as they have been raised in the twentieth century. In the years after World War I, in the wake of Germany's defeat, the October Revolution, the failed revolts in Budapest and Munich, and the economic and political upheavals of the years that ushered in Weimar, many intellectuals worried deeply about redemption and its relation to politics. We dare not ignore their reflections; at the same time, we dare not appropriate their conclusions without careful thought. How we deal with redemption in our own society and in our own times may differ significantly from how they did so, not the least because of the troubled experience of democratic society in their day. But there is much to be learned from what they thought.

Messianism and Politics in
Modernist Intellectual Culture

Both Karl Barth and Paul Tillich were, at certain stages of their early careers, vigorous and active socialists. Recent work on Barth's development while pastor in Safenwil, especially the work of Friedrich-Wilhelm Marquardt and his supporters, shows that Barth was a labor organizer, an opponent of private property, and an engaged religious leader as early as 1911 and indeed throughout his years in the practical ministry.[3] Even as late as 1919, after the publication of the first edition of his commentary on *Romans,* Barth publicly voiced his commitment to the active political life in his lecture "The Christian's Place in Society."[4] Barth finds the ground of the Christian life in a Beyond that directs the Christian's here-and-now, but there is no question in his mind that the Christian's place is indeed in the world and in society. "Society is not left wholly to itself. Married life and the family, civilization and the economic order, art and science, the state, the party, and international relations not only take their familiar course in accordance with the laws of their own logical inner workings but are also at least modified by another factor full of promise. That their familiar course is a wrong one is plainer to our eyes than formerly. The catastrophe from which we are emerging but are not yet free has brought this fact for many, though not for all, into devastating clearness."[5] To Barth, of course, the Christian's capacity, direction, and principles come from God, but in part what they yield is what he calls not a "standpoint" but rather "an instant in a *movement,*" a "movement from above," "the movement of God in history."[6] What this leads to is a "new life." "The Wholly Other in God . . . drives us with compelling power to look for a basic, ultimate, original correlation between our life and that wholly other life."[7] And this occurs through a criticism of society that draws on the Christian's being in the world that is also a being in a renewed, immediate relation to God, the Wholly Other. This is Barth's view in 1919. By then he had become a member of the Social Democratic Party; later he would oppose Nazism and become, as is well-known, a leader of the Church opposition to Hitler and Nazi fascism. To be sure, his political and moral involvement can be seen to have limitations, certainly with respect to the Jewish people, but this does not compromise the fact that while he saw redemption as ultimately God's to grant—"God alone can save the world,"[8] he still took the demand within God's revelation to direct the Christian to a broadly socialist political agenda.

And this sense of demandedness was also true for Paul Tillich, whose commitment to socialism in the Weimar years was clear and vigorous. It grew out of his experience during the war as a chaplain on the front lines, where the horrific suffering, pain, and despair that he had experienced led him to breakdowns on more than one occasion, and destroyed his optimism. He became aware of the evils brought about by militarism, capitalism, and class division, and so, when the war ended, he sought out common spirits and joined others in the "*Kairos* circle," a small group of Christian and Jewish intellectuals who appreciated the time as rich in need and possibility.[9] The word *Kairos* "signifies a moment of time filled with unconditioned meaning and demand. . . . Kairos is the fulfilled moment of time in which the present and the future, the holy that is given and the holy that is demanded meet, and from whose concrete tensions the new creation proceeds in which sacred import is realized in necessary form. Prophetism is consciousness of Kairos. . . . "[10] Prophetism, moreover, is "the religious unity of morality and the metaphysics of history" and hence the core of religious socialism. Its aim is "a condition in which the spiritual and social forms are filled with the import of the Unconditional as the foundation, meaning, and reality of all forms."[11] For Tillich, this is a social, communal goal. "Religious socialism is a community of those who understand themselves in the consciousness of the Kairos and who struggle" for the realization of this goal—no matter what their party, confession, or movement.

Tillich, in this essay, published in the journal of the "*Kairos* circle" in 1923, began to work out for himself a rapprochement between Christianity and socialism. In the spring of 1919, when he began teaching at the University of Berlin, his first lecture course was titled "Christianity and the Present Social Problem." It was a theme that persisted for Tillich throughout the decade, as he continued his reflections about the principles of socialism and then, in the fateful year 1933, published his results, *The Socialist Decision*. In a sense, the book was belated; it had no effect, for its most diabolical nemesis had come to power before it could be published. It nonetheless reveals Tillich's continued commitment to the continuity between Christian ideals and socialist action.[12]

We might expect that professional religious leaders and trained theologians would have considered deeply the relation between social and political involvement and the ideals of Christianity. These were and continue to be staples of religious discussion. It is in other areas, however, where the complications arise most vividly, especially for Jewish thought and Jewish life.

The relation between artistic creativity and everyday, bourgeois life is both an analogue of our problem and also a particularly profound instance of it. In these early decades of the century, with its aestheticism and neo-Romanticism, art in all its forms played for many a quasi-religious role, and when artistic experience was viewed as a surrogate for religious experience, many took artistic activity—painting, writing, and performance—as itself redemptive. It was not generally viewed as a vehicle of communal or social salvation, to be sure, and hence not as utopian or messianic in any pure sense, but it was certainly conceived as an avenue for personal fulfillment and transcendence. As we have seen, one of the most common, pervasive themes of the period, among artists of all kinds, is the trauma of the struggle between the life of the artist and everyday, domestic, bourgeois life.

Often the struggle between the artist's special task and domestic life took a sexual form. Georg Lukács's early intellectual passion was drama and the study of drama. As a young man, in Budapest, during the middle years of the century's first decade, Lukács was deeply involved in avant garde theater. Budapest, however, was hardly a center of artistic creativity, and so, Lukács decided to move to Berlin where he studied with Simmel in Berlin. After a sojourn back in Hungary, he, along with Ernst Bloch, became members of Max

Weber's circle in Heidelberg, where he made plans to write a dissertation on aesthetics but also became immersed in the study of Dostoyevsky. From 1908 to 1911, Lukács wrote essays on a number of
poets, novelists, and dramatists, whose work reflected the contemporary crisis of culture and life. In 1908, the year in which Lukács
had an affair with the young painter Irma Seidler, he conceived of
himself as an artist and writer, and saw his dilemma, sexual and
erotic, as the incommensurability of bourgeois society and the life
of the artist.

In his diaries of those years and in his essay on Kierkegaard,
Lukács portrayed that struggle. "Kierkegaard's heroism was that he
wanted to create forms from life. His honesty was that he saw the
crossroads and journeyed to the end of the road he had chosen. His
tragedy was that he wanted to live what cannot be lived. . . . The
poet's life has no meaning and value because it is never absolute,
never a thing in itself and for itself."[13] To Lukács, Kierkegaard was
an artist and a poet, his religious choice like that of the artist.
Hence, Kierkegaard's heroism, honesty, and tragedy all concern the
challenge facing the true artist, to bring form to life, to limit the
unlimited. Adopting the language of "life" from Simmel and ultimately from *Lebensphilosophie,* Lukács saw culture, art and religion
as the expression of a drive or force, which he called "life," to ob-
jectify itself. But this is ultimately a "tragic" situation, since "form"
was in itself the antithesis of "life." Hence, to the poet, creativity
can only achieve absoluteness in poetry, not in the world of the
everyday. For such a person, existence is an either-or. So it was for
Lukács himself, in these early years. Like Kierkegaard, he could love
his calling or Irma Seidler but not both; his was a choice between
love and the formal relationship of marriage and, for him, there was
no choice. He chose his art, left Irma Seidler, and later grieved her
suicide. The redemptive was not to be realized in the everyday; it
was an alternative to it.[14]

The same tension marked the life and work of Franz Kafka, but
with Kafka its forms are more varied and deeper. Kafka's erotic life
too has this character; Kafka's five-year relationship with Felice
Bauer, confessional, tortured, passionate but virtually monastic all

at once, exhibits the tension between Kafka's commitment to his authorship and his longing for love and personal intimacy. This is what Elias Canetti calls "Kafka's other trial," an estrangement and tormented existence that forces itself to live at a distance from what it hungers for. As early as 1912, Canetti comments, Kafka "begins to sense that Felice is a danger to him" and that she threatens "his solitary nights" and thereby "the solitude of writing."[15] Kafka could not devote himself to his writing and to Felice Bauer at the same time, unless, that is, his relationship with her took the shape of writing, a long, monumental epistolary accomplishment that in part became a surrogate for genuine interpersonal intimacy and for much more.

But Kafka's struggle between his art and everyday bourgeois life took other forms as well. At a mundane level, it was reflected in his acknowledged unhappiness about having to spend so much of his time at work for the Worker's Accident Insurance Company of Bohemia, where he used his legal and analytical skills to prepare elaborate reports on strategies for industrial accident prevention. At a deeper level, the struggle was reflected in his strained relationship with some members of his family and especially with his father. There were many dimensions, of course, to this father-son relationship, but one certainly involved his father's dismissal of and even disdain for all those things that Kafka found rewarding and important, including his friendship with Yitzhak Löwy, the Yiddish actor, his engagements with Felice Bauer and with Julie Wohryzek, his growing interest in Judaism and especially East European Jewish life, and ultimately his writing. In Kafka's famous letter to his father of 1919, he recalled his father's rude dismissal of his book *In the Penal Colony*, an act that exemplified to him the rift that had always separated his father from himself. Indeed, as Kafka put it, his writing was always about his father.[16] There is no better evidence for this than two of Kafka's earliest and most powerful stories, "The Judgment" and "Metamorphosis," both of which can be read as reflections on the estrangement that existed between the artistic son and his father and on the eventual death of one side of the son as he struggled to reconcile his writing with his yearning for his father's acknowledgment and love. And what appeared earliest in these stories recurred again and again in Kafka's works, in stories such as "The Hunger Artist," "Report to an Academy," and "Josephine the Mouse Singer," stories one strand of which always signifies the tension between the artist and the world to which he is never wholly reconciled.

If art, writing, and authorship, then, are routes to individual fulfillment and salvation, their relationship to everyday life is fraught with difficulty. If we follow Rilke and Kafka and so many others of this period, we must see them as deeply incommensurable. Everyday life, history, the political in the broadest sense, these are divorced from the redemptive; they are alternatives; one cannot live both. To do so, as Georg Lukács puts it, is to try to live what cannot be lived.

In Lukács, these issues become social and political. Immediately after the war began in 1914, disgusted by the enthusiastic support he saw among so many of his teachers and friends, Lukács returned to Budapest and published the introduction to his work on Dostoyevsky as a short book, *The Theory of the Novel*. Adopting a sociological examination of literary genre, together with a philosophy of history indebted to Fichte, Lukács described the modern world as the world of the novel, an "epoch of absolute sinfulness," of disenchantment and alienation. In the book's final pages, however, he noticed hints of a world to come, a world with the "form of the renewed epic," communal, organic, whole. It is a world intimated in the novels of Tolstoy and, most of all, Dostoyevsky. Indeed, in Dostoyevsky this world is more than intimated; it "is drawn for the first time simply as a seen reality."[17] In other words, Dostoyevsky is a kind of prophet of this redemptive goal but one whose message Lukács only hesitatingly eulogizes in the famous final words of his book:

Only formal analysis of [Dostoyevsky's] works can show whether he is already the Homer or the Dante of that world or whether he merely supplies the songs which, together with the songs of other forerunners, later artists will one day weave into a great unity: whether he is merely a beginning or already a completion. It will then be the task of historico-philosophical interpretation to decide whether we

> are really about to leave the age of absolute sinfulness or whether the
> new has no other herald but our hopes: those hopes are signs of a
> world to come, still so weak that it can easily be crushed by the sterile
> power of the merely existent.[18]

Here history has a shape and a goal, but there is no recognition of
the role of political action in realizing that goal. Lukács's complete
attention is given to the artistic expression of the world, without
any dialectical appreciation of the ways that art and world interact
and without any causal attention to the political, social, and economic events that give it shape.

As the decade wore on, Lukács became increasingly involved in
socialism and Marxism and, after the Russian revolution in 1917,
considered seriously membership in the Communist Party. In 1918,
he debated with himself and expressed his doubts in a paper, "Bolshevism as a Moral Problem," but by the time it was published in
late 1918 he had already made his choice in favor of membership.[19]
The essay is nonetheless revealing, especially in light of the issues we
are discussing, for it raised in a vivid way the question about how
the redemptive is related to history and the political.

Lukács's thinking had taken a certain kind of turn. Earlier, like
Rilke, Kafka, and others, he had denied that personal salvation
through art or mysticism or any such vehicle could occur in the
everyday world; ordinary life could not facilitate salvation. In 1915,
in *The Theory of the Novel*, he had appropriated from Fichte a philosophy of history and from Simmel a sociological account of how
literary form expresses the essential features of historical periods.
Still, utopia and history were causally insulated. By 1918, he had
changed his mind. If the goal of history is a pure community, then
politics was certainly the means to achieve it and had to be, if it was
history itself that was to be transformed and redeemed. The question was the *limits* of such political action; does this redemptive
goal justify *any* political means, no matter how horrific or immoral?
Could one, as he puts it in this essay, lie one's way through to the
truth? And Lukács answers, no; morality had an autonomy about it;
goodness could not be corrupted in order to be achieved. But by
the time the essay was published, Lukács had changed his mind and

joined the Communist Party, which, he had come to believe, was the appropriate agent for historical change and which could do whatever it must in order to achieve its goals. If history dictated that the class struggle and capitalism would have to suffer a revolution and if that revolution was to lead through a dictatorship of the proletariat, then so be it. The ultimate goal was worth it and the means were necessary and unavoidable.

To see history this way was to see it dialectically, to allow for a negative stage that would give rise ultimately to a positive goal. It was also, of course, to treat political or historical action as causally required for historical development and hence for the realization of the utopian future. Some would agree with the latter, however, but not with the former. Buber and Cohen, for example, both took political action to contribute to the messianic future, to an ideal society of justice, peace, and harmony. While they differed in some ways, both agreed on this, that ideal human community was to be realized in the world by real human beings and through cultivation of real human relationships that were just, humane, and morally exemplary. Lukács's dialectical view of historical development, however, accepted violence and suffering as necessary for the ultimate socialist state; to Cohen, the means had to be as morally humane as the goal; to Buber, too, the means and end had to be commensurate, although for him they were both conceived in terms of humane and just interpersonal relationships rather than in terms of the moral law and moral intentions.

In the period after World War I, then, there were many who conceived of redemption as a communal and social goal. Some took that goal to require historical and political action to bring it about; others did not see the redemptive as continuous with the political. To some, redemption was the culmination of human action; to others it was its dialectical outcome through opposition. What the debates of these years reveal clearly is the problematic in all its ramifications: are life, politics, and history radically severed from redemption and eternity, or are they somehow connected? Whatever their answers, these thinkers certainly bequeathed to us this question.

Messianism and the Political in Judaism

It is a question very familiar as well to traditional Jewish thinking about history and messianism. The midrashic and Talmudic texts that display the tension between history and the coming of the Messiah are well known. In some, the coming of the Messiah is associated with human goodness and accomplishment, in others with human suffering and immorality. In some, the Messiah will come when human beings have done all they could to better the world, in others when they have accomplished as much evil as the world can bear. In some, people are enjoined to wait patiently for the Messiah with prayer and anticipation, in others to work untiringly to prepare for the messianic arrival.[20]

In his recent magisterial account of messianism and the Kabbalah, Moshe Idel notes that this tension is already Biblical; he cites Jon Levenson who "has described two different tendencies . . . which are found in the biblical corpus: the royal ideology and the Sinaitic one. The former is concerned with divine intervention in history, while the latter emphasizes the effect of the performance of the divine commandments."[21] Idel nicely goes on to summarize the ways in which this polarity occurs in Talmudic literature:

> There is a certain proclivity to attribute the beginning of the messianic era to the moral behavior of the generation. Extreme pictures of the human deprivation that will precede the advent of the Messiah—or, on the contrary, the merits that characterize humanity in that generation—are attempts to attenuate the unexpected coming of the redeemer and to portray it as an event unrelated to religious activity. In this literature it is religious behavior that determines the advent, not the unknown, 'irrational' divine decree, as in some of the rabbinic sources. The reference to the merits or sins of the Jews as a condition for the advent or deferral of the messianic era is intended to align the messianic outbursts with a more predictable behavior, which at the same time reinforces the importance of the ritual as the most sublime form of behavior.

As Idel summarizes these rabbinic reflections, then, there were some who emphasized "the unknown grounded in the divine" and hence had a more apocalyptic character and others who aimed at "forms of religiosity which strive more toward instruction about a stable, or at least perfectible, order."[22]

Some rabbis, for example, speak of a cycle of catastrophe, renewal and further catastrophe, only after which the Messiah will come, a cycle including flood and drought, famine that will lead to widespread death and the forgetting of the Torah, great recovery that will lead to satiety, rejoicing, and the return of Torah, and finally war.[23] Rabbi Judah says that the generation in which the Messiah comes will be marked by prostitution, desolation, refugees wandering the land, defamation and rejection of the teachings of scribes and sages, and the lacking of truth.[24] It will also be marked by turmoil and disrespect between relatives; Rabbi Nehorai said that "young men will insult the old, and old men will stand before the young [to give them honor]; daughters will rise up against their mothers, and daughters-in-law against their mothers-in-law."[25] Indeed, evil will be so extreme that Rabbi Isaac said: "The son of David will not come until the whole world is converted to the belief of the heretics."[26] At the very same time, however, that the rabbis speak of the messianic age as dialectically related to the evils of history and the world, they also acknowledge the need for some human contribution, even if it is not by itself sufficient to be messianic. On this view, there is continuity between what human beings accomplish and what God alone completes, albeit a continuity with a gap between contribution and culmination. As Rav said, for example, all the dates for the final redemption have passed; now it depends upon "repentance and good deeds."[27] And although there was a subsequent dispute about the role of repentance, there is a good deal of support for the necessity of good deeds, from generosity and charity to the avoidance of pride. The upshot of these texts is the tension I referred to earlier, between the necessity of human action and its fruitlessness. Rabbi Jochanan said: "The son of David will come only in a generation that is either altogether righteous or altogether wicked."[28]

Whatever the practical implications of such diverse views, their overall impact is to pose the question of the commensurability of politics and messianism in a vivid and powerful way. It is no surprise to find the question reiterated and ramified throughout the subsequent history of Jewish and Christian reflection on history, divine providence, and the redemption of humankind.

Two Dimensions: This Worldly Redemption and Politics as a Means

If we return to the European intellectual milieu prior to and following World War I and specifically to thinkers engaged to one degree or other in reflecting on these issues of redemption and utopia with Judaism in mind, we do well to focus on two dimensions of the problem we have identified, on two dimensions of the issue of continuity. The first is whether the redemptive goal is taken to be a this-worldly one, in some way a transformation of human society and human life as we know it. The second is whether political and social action is seen as contributing in some significant way to the redemptive accomplishment.[29]

The fact that Martin Buber's famous and influential lectures to the Prague Bar Kochba Society, delivered in the years 1908–1911, represent the intermingling of his mystical understanding of Judaism with his Zionism already suggests that for him somehow Jewish destiny and political action were intimately connected. In 1899–1901 Buber had been in Berlin, studying among others with Dilthey and Simmel, and there he became associated with a small group dedicated to the conceptualization and realization of genuine communities. Founded by the brothers Heinrich and Julius Hart and led in practice by Gustav Landauer, this group, the *Neue Gemeinschaft* (New Community), provided a setting for discussion about the nature of genuine community and the tactics for its realization. Landauer wrote extensively on socialism, became a student of Fritz Mauthner's philosophy of language, was a translator of Meister Eckhart, and ultimately was the victim of a brutal assassination during the Munich revolution. He and the new communitarians influenced Buber's conception of Zionism as a movement of Jewish renewal whose social goal was the development of ideal human community.

In his second Prague lecture, in 1910, Buber proposed that Jewish destiny involves a "striving for unity" which aimed to realize unity in the world—"for unity within individual man; for unity between divisions of the nation, and between nations; for unity between mankind and every living being; and for unity between God and the world."[30] Buber calls this striving "the primal process within the Jew" and associates it, socially, with the striving for universal justice within each nation and internationally with "the Messianic ideal, which later . . . was reduced in scope, made finite, and called socialism."[31] Here, then, in Buber we find the same this-worldly conception of an international socialism that one finds, say, in Hermann Cohen, in Barth, Tillich, Landauer, and in so many others of the age. To be sure, different thinkers were more or less attuned to nuance, and were more or less politically savvy and hence aware of the finer economic and political issues associated with political theory of a more practical kind. But my point is that Buber shared with many others the basic conviction that the messianic ideal was not an other-worldly abstraction, a utopian vision, but rather a this-worldly program. To call the ideal "eternity" was not to detach it from history, time, and the world; it was to associate it with God, with divine purpose, and to indicate clearly that unlike the remainder of history which was always not-yet, always changing and undergoing transformation and development and regression, this ideal human community would be, when realized, in a sense "timeless" and permanent, or at least as much as one could hope for in the world. Buber, of course, differed with Barth in thinking, at least in 1912, that Jews would be the vanguard of this movement to social community and that humankind could achieve it. For Barth, this was the Christian's task and ultimately only God could realize it. Nonetheless, they shared with many others the commitment to its realizability.

This worldly realizability of the messianic ideal was, of course, a centerpiece of Hermann Cohen's view of the Jewish contribution to ethics, and it was only one of the things that he passed on to his foremost Jewish student, Franz Rosenzweig.[32] Part of Rosenzweig's genius was to graft this conception of a kind of international socialism onto the trunk of a tree shaped by his own appropriation of Friedrich Meinecke's views about nationalism and cosmopolitanism. In a sense, Rosenzweig had come to think, by 1910, that Bismarckian Germany was not to achieve that synthesis of politics and morality that Hegel had anticipated and Meinecke had thought was being realized in the Second German Reich.[33] The events of 1914 only confirmed Rosenzweig in his skepticism, and by 1917, when he began to think about bringing together his views about Judaism, Christianity, history, and philosophy, he was sure that the messianic ideal was still in the future. Judaism and Christianity were two avenues to it, one via political action, the other through ritual anticipation. But the crucial point for us is that his conception of eternity or redemption always had a decidedly this-worldly character. When, in *The Star of Redemption* (1921), he described redemption in terms of an intimate, face-to-face community, the outcome of an interpersonal love that is the human response to God's love for human beings, he was placing himself within a group of thinkers of his day who felt similarly that the only redemption worth anticipating was one that fulfilled human social existence.[34]

Among these thinkers, I believe, were Gershom Scholem and Walter Benjamin, life-long friends, of course, and, in the period we are talking about, during and immediately after the war, close intellectual partners. When they first met in July of 1915, as we have noted, both were opposed to the war; both had broken with Buber's intuitive, mystical style of Judaism; both had been active in the German youth movement and then left it. With them we confront directly the second of our questions, whether human political action contributes to the messianic end.

Benjamin had once been active in the intellectual wing of the German youth movement and had been especially influenced by the educational reformer Gustav Wyneken.[35] In 1912, Benjamin had clarified his own sense of cultural Judaism in distinction to Buber's experiential, mystical approach; he had come to see Judaism as the bearer of European culture and spirituality, and he also saw the writer as the embodiment of the Jewish status as outsider and critic. He was devastated by the war; its horror led him to break with his mentor Wyneken, who supported the war, like so many others, and when two close friends, Paul Heinle and Rivka Seligson, committed suicide in despair over the war, he abandoned all hope for the youth movement and was confirmed in his conviction that no messianic era was imminent. Later, in "A Berlin Chronicle" (1932), Benjamin would refer to the Meeting House where Heinle and Seligson had died as "the strictest pictorial expression of the point in history occupied by this last true elite of bourgeois Berlin," a location "close to the abyss of the Great War." He recalled their "final, heroic attempt to change the attitudes of people without changing their circumstances. We did not know that it was bound to fail, but there was hardly one of us whose resolve such knowledge could have altered."[36] In 1917, Benjamin fled his draft notice by moving to Switzerland, settled in Berne, and spent most of the summer talking with Scholem; their conversations ranged over a variety of topics, from Kant and a metaphysics of experience to the mystical theory of language we discussed earlier.

Scholem had rebelled against his totally assimilated Jewish home and, vitalized by Buber's Prague lectures, turned to the study of Hebrew and the Talmud. During the war years, he joined the Zionist youth group *Jung-Juda* in Berlin and became its spokesperson and leader. But his Zionism led Scholem to oppose the war, and in 1915 he was expelled from school for signing an anti-war letter. Buber invited Scholem to meet, but Scholem was incensed by Buber's mystical Zionism and his support for the war.[37] When, in 1917, his brother Werner was jailed for his anti-war activism, Scholem became totally alienated from his father and moved into a pension in Berlin that was the home of many East European Jews, including Salman Rubaschoff and Schmuel Yosef Agnon. By 1918, when he met Benjamin in Berne, he had turned to the study of mathematics, but within a year Scholem would make the decision to move to Munich to study Kabbalah.

The relationship between messianism and politics was one of the themes of the conversations between Benjamin and Scholem. There is a document in Benjamin's corpus that deals specifically with this subject; it will help us to identify the options discussed by the two friends, options that are still importantly accessible to us today. This text, which we discussed in Chapter 2, is now called a "Theologico-Political Fragment."[38] It is a brief page-long piece that, I believe, is the nucleus of a review of Ernst Bloch's *Geist der Utopie* (Spirit of Utopia), a work that it mentions explicitly.

Bloch's book was published first in 1918, and in a letter to Scholem of September 15, 1919, Benjamin mentions and briefly comments on the book. A few days later, on September 19, he reports to Ernst Schoen about his thinking concerning Bloch and his book:

> I have done a lot of thinking on my own and, in so doing, have conceived of ideas that are so clear that I hope to be able to write them down soon. They concern politics. In many respects—not only in this one—a friend's book has proven useful. He is the only person of consequence I have gotten to know in Switzerland thus far. . . . The book is called *Spirit of Utopia* [*Geist der Utopie*] by Ernst Bloch. It exhibits enormous deficiencies. Nonetheless, I am indebted to the book for much that is substantive, and the author is ten times better than his book. . . . the author stands alone and philosophically stands up for his cause, while almost everything we read today of a philosophical nature written by our contemporaries is derivative and adulterated. You can never get a handle on its moral center and, at the most, it leads you to the origin of the evil that it itself represents.[39]

By November 23, Benjamin wrote to Scholem that the plan to write a review of the book had "come to naught" because the book, with his marginalia, had been misplaced; presumably it was found, for on December 5, he wrote to Schoen that he was beginning a lengthy review of it. He was still at work on the review in January 1920 when he wrote to Scholem and indicated one of his foci, the diagnosis of esoteric language; by early February it was complete, but it was never published and eventually was lost.[40]

As Anson Rabinbach has argued, Benjamin's differences with Bloch were dramatic and they focused on politics. Bloch had become a socialist and was deeply involved in the revolutionary movements of 1918–1919. Benjamin had little sympathy; in these years he was antipolitical and vigorous in his denial of political activism as necessarily tainted by violence.[41] "Benjamin considered the problem of revolution from the heights of a messianic philosophy of history that in principle rejected any intrinsic relationship between 'activism' and utopia."[42]

This *rupture* between political, historical action and messianism is a central theme of the "Fragment." "Only the Messiah himself consummates all history, in the sense that he alone redeems, completes, creates its relation to the Messianic. For this reason nothing historical can relate itself on its own account to anything Messianic. . . . Therefore the order of the profane cannot be built up on the idea of the Divine Kingdom, and therefore theocracy has no political, but only a religious meaning."[43] History and politics are the domain of violence and the catastrophic; they prepare for the Messianic but do not contribute to it or bring it about. In 1919–1920 Benjamin is a political pessimist, although one with a hope for the messianic redemption. What there is in the meantime is a sure movement toward self-destruction and, at the same time, the work of the philosophical critic of language, texts, and culture, a task that may bring illumination but one that will not bring redemption.

In his influential paper of 1959, "Toward an Understanding of the Messianic Idea in Judaism," Scholem invoked this catastrophic or disruptive view of the messianic era and used it to characterize traditional Jewish messianic thinking in the Talmud and beyond. "The redemption which is born here is in no causal sense a result of previous history. It is precisely the lack of transition between history and the redemption which is always stressed by the prophets and apocalyptists. . . . there can be no preparation for the Messiah. He comes suddenly, unannounced, and precisely when he is least expected or when hope has long been abandoned."[44] One stand of messianic thinking in Judaism, as Scholem sees it, adopts the kind of disruptive view that grips Benjamin, consummate in his modernism, in the years after the Great War. Politics and history are the domain of the profane, of violence, pain, and suffering. Messianic thinking looks forward to a better day but not one to which political action contributes—except insofar as politics creates a situation so horrific that only something utterly opposed to it could possibly redeem it. Politics, as the domain of Hobbesian individuals, of competition, aggression, and war, only contributes to the realization of a utopia by creating its negation. But this is only one strand of Jewish messianic thinking. There are others.

At the end of his essay, Scholem turned briefly to a reflection on the implications of this conception and delivered a critique. "In Judaism the Messianic idea has compelled a *life lived in deferment,* in which nothing can be done definitively, nothing can be irrevocably accomplished. One may say, perhaps, the Messianic idea is the real anti-existentialist idea. Precisely understood, there is nothing concrete which can be accomplished by the unredeemed. This makes for the greatness of Messianism, but also for its constitutional weakness." And Scholem was very specific about that weakness and what the modern Jewish antidote might be. He speaks of a "modern Jewish readiness for irrevocable action in the concrete realm, when it set out on the utopian return to Zion," and he notes that "it is a readiness which no longer allows itself to be fed on hopes. Born out of the horror and destruction that was Jewish history in our generation, it is bound to history itself and not to meta-history. . . . "[45] In muted but unwavering terms, Scholem alludes to Jewish political activism, in response to the horrors of Nazi fascism, in behalf of the creation of a Jewish state. In short, Scholem points to the Zionist return of Judaism into history.[46]

Clearly, Scholem focused on Benjamin's conception only to reject it. Scholem implies—and perhaps more than implies—that a Judaism lived today with pride and dignity and with a sense of responsibility cannot adopt Benjamin's disruptive view. The problematic of redemption and history must be answered in one way only; utopia is achievable but only by concrete human action. In this conviction Scholem is not alone, nor is he without opponents.

Benjamin's Later Thoughts on Messianism and History

In the thirties, Benjamin developed what we might call a kind of "intellectual activism" or, in Habermas's famous terms, a conception of "redemptive critique." During the intervening years, of course,

Benjamin had become increasingly attracted to Marxism and to dialectical materialism; at the same time, under the particular inspiration of his reading of surrealism and figures such as Eduard Fuchs, he had shaped a provocative, illuminating approach to cultural and literary criticism. Several of his literary projects exemplify this approach, at times in the service of his special style of Marxist principles. This is especially true, of course, of the famous unfinished Arcades project, intended as a redemptive investigation of the roots of bourgeois capitalism and the growth of Paris as the urban locus of its emergence and development. The understanding of his method and its philosophical foundations is laid out in the posthumously published fragments on the philosophy of history, which Benjamin carried with him at the time of his suicide.

In these fragments, Benjamin retains from his earlier thinking the belief that history is not a stream, a linear development, or a narrative whole. Rather it is episodic and discontinuous. There is no particular a priori pattern into which events and actions fit. Each present situation appears to us in a variety of ways, to some of us with greater clarity and appreciation, to some with less; to some as episodes of injustice, oppression, and suffering, to others as elements or components of a story of success and achievement. The past appears in the same ways. To the tyrants and despots of today, it appears as a story of growth and development; to the oppressed masses, the plot differs. Episodes that are billed in standard histories as revolutionary accomplishments are seen from a different perspective; their subterranean message is one of persecution, torture, manipulation, and all that results from them. Benjamin's verdict needs to be underscored, that history in fact possesses no pattern at all. Rather history is a mass of contemporary evidence—texts, monuments, buildings, artifacts, and more—that have a "past-directedness" about them, dimensions of meaning that call forth earlier times, places, and so forth. But there are no historical patterns or stories. Not only are the standard narratives of the past to be jettisoned, but also new ones as well. In their place, we should seek a different type of understanding of both the past and the present, a *non-narrative understanding,* an insight given over to depth and clarification via juxtaposition and archeology rather than causal explanation and narration.

Let us focus on three aspects of Benjamin's innovative kind of historical understanding. One concerns the motivation for historical inquiry. The second concerns the method itself. The third concerns the outcome of that method and its contribution, if there is one, to redemptive change.

Why investigate the past? Like Nietzsche, in his famous attack on scientific historiography and antiquarianism, Benjamin believes that history begins with the present and with an appreciation of the dangers or urgencies of the present.[47] In short, history is always in terms of the present; historical inquiry is always based on relevance to the present. In his theses on the concept of history, Benjamin acknowledges that the present is a time of danger. He notes that "we" live in a "state of emergency" which needs to be trumpeted and understood and that this "state of emergency" involves "the struggle against fascism."[48] Every present, then, offers "a revolutionary chance in the fight for the oppressed past" which is also a revolutionary chance in the fight for the oppressed present as well.[49] Benjamin's Marxism, then, pictures this struggle against Fascism as the way the "class struggle" was manifest in the late thirties. Brilliantly, Benjamin synthesizes the shadow of threat that hangs over both the present world and the past: "To articulate the past historically . . . means to seize hold of a memory as it flashes up at a moment of danger. . . . The danger affects both the content of the tradition and its receivers. The same threat hangs over both: that of becoming a tool of the ruling classes . . . *even the dead* will not be safe from the enemy if he wins."[50] The same threat, the same danger, is there for Benjamin and his contemporaries and for the past, the tradition, history; if fascism is victorious, then it will dominate and oppress both. The same suffering and atrocity will affect the victims of his day and will victimize and distort their past. This, then, is what motivates historical thinking and a return to the past; it is to redeem the present and the past, both at once. Ultimately, then, for Benjamin, the goal of historical inquiry is messianic and redemptive.

Our second question is, what does that historical inquiry involve? How does the historical thinker proceed? We have already said something about this in an earlier chapter. Benjamin recommends that evidence from the past be investigated, artifacts and texts and more, in order to juxtapose a past event or epoch with our own. The central outcome of that juxtaposition and the central object of the critic's understanding is what Benjamin calls a "dialectical image" or "a unique experience with the past." "Where thinking suddenly stops in a configuration pregnant with tensions, it gives that configuration a shock, by which it crystallizes into a monad." This monad is "the constellation which [the historian's] own era has formed with a definite earlier one."[51] This is not the place to try to clarify the structure or character of these moments of "profane illumination," as Benjamin calls them in his essay on surrealism.[52] It is sufficient for us to see that for Benjamin, the objects of historical study, so to speak, are images created by juxtaposing past and present in such a way that each illuminates the other. These images are the products of association, reflection, and a kind of mutually illuminating understanding. "A Berlin Chronicle" is filled with examples as are Benjamin's works on Baudelaire and Paris in the nineteenth century.

Finally, however, we need to ask what is the ultimate goal of this kind of historical thinking. Scholem had rejected Benjamin's apocalyptic view of messianism and history in favor of a messianism causally connected to political activism. In these late fragments, as we have seen, Benjamin persists with his view of rupture or discontinuity but now sees historical thinking as a method of redemption, as "redemptive critique." In other words, the ultimate goal of Benjamin's method of cultural and literary critique must be messianic or redemptive. Indeed, time and again, he says just that. Michael Jennings, in his excellent discussion of dialectical images and Benjamin's views about language and history, puts it this way: "Dialectical images are bursts of recognition which, in revealing knowledge of a better world and a better time, may precipitate revolution."[53] Benjamin himself puts it more enigmatically. He speaks of "a secret agreement between past generations and the present one. Our coming was expected on earth. Like every generation that preceded us, we have been endowed with a *weak* Messianic power, a power to which the past has a claim."[54] Every present moment is potentially messianic and every present generation potentially redemptive. Hence, each generation can redeem its own present from suffering and injustice and oppression; it can also redeem its past; and it can contribute to the redemption of some generation yet to be born. Some past or pasts, when they were the present, already anticipated us, our need for them, and our redemption of them and of our own world. No present redeems all of history once and for all, but each redeems a great deal and then looks forward to future redemptions. Hence, by giving shape to dialectical images, the historian-critic "establishes a conception of the present as the 'time of the now' which is shot through with chips of Messianic time." Indeed, Benjamin associates this conception of every present moment as potentially redemptive with a traditional Jewish teaching, that "every second of time was the strait gate through which the Messiah might enter."[55]

Benjamin does not clearly state how the cultural and literary critic, as the genuine historian, contributes to the messianic redemption of the present world, to a victory in the struggle with fascism, to the political realization of a society of justice, peace, and equality. At one level, at least, the role of the historian is to make manifest to the oppressed the fact that they are being oppressed and to clarify how that oppression is being carried out. Hence, the critic's role is the quasi-Socratic one of showing people what their condition is, exposing ignorance, promoting self-knowledge, and hence laying bare the lineaments of oppression and injustice. It is to show those who are enslaved that they are in fact enslaved and what can and should be done to relieve their suffering and claim their dignity and self-respect. Presumably, Benjamin believes that this is the natural preparation for political action in behalf of the creation of a better world and a better life for those oppressed and that this revolution is the real redemption or the one most passionately sought. Even with a non-narrative, episodic, or disruptive view of history, then, one can take political action to contribute to the messianic.

Israel and the Holocaust: Messianism and Politics Today

In his classic essay, Scholem calls attention to the Zionist commitment to Jewish dignity and to the way in which the return to Zion can be conceived as a response in action to the suffering and destruction that we associate with Auschwitz. His remarks are similar to those of many Zionists and to several post-Holocaust theologians, both Jewish and Christian, who claim that any authentic response to the Holocaust must involve a commitment to Israel's survival that is in its own way messianic.[56] It is a view found in the work of Christian theologians like Franklin Littell, A. Roy Eckardt, and Paul van Buren and in Jewish theologians like Irving Greenberg and Emil Fackenheim. To some, a commitment to Israel's maintenance and survival, then, is both messianic and political, a proper response of those who continue to believe in Jewish redemptive goals in a world where the confidence in God's redeeming power has been destroyed or is at least attenuated.

For Jean Améry, who was born a Jew but brought up a Catholic, there never existed such confidence; he came under the influence of Sartre, became wholly secular and participated in the French underground. Caught and tortured by the Nazis, Améry eventually was sent to Auschwitz. Later, after the war and the Holocaust, he would recall his earlier recognition, while sitting in a café in Vienna in 1935, that in virtue of the Nuremberg laws he was a Jew, whether he wanted to be or not, and for that reason a "dead man on furlough."[57] He survived Auschwitz with a sense that the only authentic way to respond to Nazi persecution was to strike back, to feel a sense of solidarity with all those whose human dignity is under assault, and hence to identify with Israel as representative of those engaged in a "political" defense of human dignity and respect. This solidarity with Israel, he came to think, was a hallmark of what he describes as a "catastrophe Judaism." Améry exemplifies a version of Zionism that is a moral-political response to Nazi atrocity that constitutes a kind of secular Judaism, active and redemptive but wholly severed from religious sensibility. He refers to this twin reality, his commitment to struggle for human dignity wherever it is assaulted in response to the Nazi attempt to extinguish human worth and self-respect and his inability to identify with Jewish religious sensibility, as "the impossibility and necessity" of his being a Jew. In a sense, Améry's Judaism is an anomaly, of course, given its distance from Jewish practices, learning, and tradition, but it does show one way in which Judaism after Auschwitz, even if wholly secular, can be both political and redemptive at once.

There is no incautious, self-righteous optimism in Améry; his Judaism and his Zionism are realistic and sober. He treats the Zionist and Jewish return to historical, political self-assertion as a necessity, as noble perhaps but not as an expression of self-indulgence. This realism marks many of the post-Holocaust responses to Israel. Paul Van Buren, for example, reminds Christians that the Zionist return to historical self-assertion and political autonomy is truly remarkable and transforming for Christianity's understanding of its relationship with the Jewish people. Perhaps Van Buren is insufficiently attentive to the importance of Christian guilt for the horrors of Nazism; his rethinking of a Christian theology of the Jewish people is grounded less in the Holocaust and Christian responsibility than it is in this recognition of the political role of the Jewish people in Israel and hence in the awareness of Israel as a locus of power in history. Theologians like Roy Eckardt, Franklin Littell, and David Tracy focus on the Holocaust and its implications for the church and its sense of its relationship to the Jewish people, but all recognize as well the importance of Israel as a commitment to Jewish survival and to the notion of a Jewish homeland.

Among Jewish theologians, Emil Fackenheim has labored to clarify the religious and the secular dimensions of the Zionist project in a post-Holocaust world. For Fackenheim, Jewish life requires of itself a return into history, and that return is exemplified importantly by the creation, defense, and development of the state of Israel. From the early seventies, for thirty years, Fackenheim has discussed the role of Israel in a world after Auschwitz; we cannot and need not deal with the development and extent of his writings here.

One feature of his thinking, however, is especially relevant to our discussion of messianism and politics. Fackenheim pointedly refuses to join the two events, the death camps and the renewal of the state of Israel, in an explanatory way. In an important paper, "The Holocaust and the State of Israel: Their Relation," he argues that the Holocaust resists explanation, historical or theological; the event has no meaning or purpose. It fits no intellectual pattern; the responsible intellectual encounter with the death camps does not yield satisfaction, understanding, or what we might call "intellectual accommodation." Fackenheim then turns to the two events together: "What holds true of the Holocaust holds true also of its connection with the state of Israel. Here too the explaining mind suffers ultimate failure. *Yet it is necessary, not only to perceive a bond between the two events but also so to act as to make it unbreakable.* . . . Such a bond is *possible* because to seek a *cause* or a *meaning* is one thing, to give a *response* is another. And it is necessary because the heart of every *authentic* response to the Holocaust—religious or secularist, Jewish and non-Jewish—is a commitment to the autonomy and security of the state of Israel."[58] For Fackenheim, then, a commitment to the survival of the Jewish state is somehow integral to a genuine and serious response to Auschwitz. Later in the essay he will characterize the features of that response as "a fervent believing, turned by despair from patient waiting into heroic acting" or, in other words, action performed in behalf of a this-worldly messianic goal.[59] It is this combination of believing and acting that manifests both the secular and the religious dimensions of the response and hence what makes it "paradigmatic" for what post-Holocaust necessity requires of the Jew. Fackenheim puts this very clearly in an earlier work, *Encounters Between Judaism and Modern Philosophy*, published in 1973:

> The Holocaust Kingdom murdered religious and secular Jews alike. . . . Only by virtue of radical "secular" self-reliance that acts as though the God who once saved could save no more can even the most "religious" survivor hold fast either to the Sinaitic past or to the Messianic future. And only by virtue of a radical "religious" memory and hope can even the most "secularist" survivor rally either the courage or the motivation to decide to remain a Jew, when every

natural impulse tempts him to seek forgetfulness and even bare safety
elsewhere. . . . This commingling of religiosity and secularity has
found historical embodiment in the rebirth of a Jewish State. . . .
After the Holocaust, the Israeli nation has become collectively what
the survivor is individually.[60]

As Fackenheim has seen it, then, a genuine post-Holocaust Zionism
is both secular and religious, activist, and responsive. It does not
seek to explain Israel in terms of the Nazi death camps and the
destruction of European Jewry. Instead it eschews explanation and
understanding for response. Moreover, as he writes elsewhere, that
response—filled with courage and hope and yet self-reliant and
active—is aimed at rectifying the conditions without which the
Nazi extermination could not have occurred: the murderous hatred
of Jews, Jewish powerlessness, and Jewish homelessness.[61] Zionism,
then, for Fackenheim, is exemplary of post-Holocaust Jewish life
and is also an important constituent of it; it is secular and religious
at once and also messianic and politically active. In *To Mend the
World,* his magnum opus, he calls Israel "a collective, particular Jewish response to history," a *Tikkun* [mending] that is "fragmentary"
and "laden with risk." It is "after unprecedented death, a unique
celebration of life."[62]

There are those, of course, for whom the creation and maintenance of the state of Israel is not messianic, so that for them political
action within the state does not contribute to or further the messianic project.[63] Among this group one finds both extremely Orthodox Jews for whom human political action plays no contributory
role in the messianic coming and liberal Jews for whom messianic
hopes, if they exist at all, are not Zionist but rather a matter of
morality and issues of social justice and human rights.[64] Some of
the latter have no special regard for Israel at all, although for the
past thirty years, Israel has played some role or other in the lives of
virtually all liberal American Jews. Still, there are those, among
modern liberal Jews, for whom Zionism and the state, while important, have not been central to their messianic aspirations in the
twentieth century. Suppose that one still clung to Jewish messianic
hopes but that those hopes were social and moral in a very broad

sense, involving the commitment to human dignity and worth everywhere in the world, to justice and peace, to renewing the "divine image" wherever it is to be found and wherever it is under assault. If that were the case, then, while a responsible post-Holocaust Jewish messianic impulse might very well include a commitment to Israel's maintenance and survival, it might also include a sense of engagement politically and socially with other evils—oppression and suffering throughout the world, human rights, environmental issues, and much else. Moreover, such a set of broad, social, and moral concerns might register in moments of challenge and quandary with respect to Israel itself, depending upon the particular circumstances. Still, this kind of messianic attitude would have this much sympathy with Scholem, Fackenheim, and others—that today the radical severing of messianic ideals from political action is a luxury no Jew can afford. After Auschwitz, it may be difficult to have faith in human capacity, but at the same time, as these thinkers might argue, it is equally difficult to abandon human capacity altogether. Whatever trust in God remains, it is certainly no stronger than our faith in humankind; while we struggle to regain the former, we must at least, as a temporary strategy, accept to some degree the latter.

In the reflections we examined from thinkers such as Lukács, Buber, Scholem, and Benjamin, there was a powerful tendency toward the notion of the redemptive and indeed toward the language of the messianic. Many of these thinkers too conceived of redemption as a this-worldly ideal, as a goal for human community in the world. Where they differed, most significantly, was over whether political action is either necessary or contributory to that goal. But this is not the end of the matter. There is at least one further option and other difficulties to face.

One difficulty is akin to a problem that we mentioned in Chapter 1. Tying the messianic together with the political is not without its risks. Religious fanaticism, when equipped with political power, can be and certainly has been an intolerant, ruthless combination. In early modern Europe, even in the Dutch provinces of the seventeenth century, there was often the fear that religious diversity threatened the civil security and stability. But the union of messianic commitments with political power, as one finds in Iraq, for example, is a formula for terror, violent repression, and horrible persecution of minorities. Hence, we must be careful to circumscribe the issue that we are here discussing: the issue is about an attitude or posture for individuals and congregations but not for public policy. One wants a view that encourages a Jewish commitment to social and political activism but does not underwrite the union at the national level, at the level of public policy and law, of messianic convictions and governmental power. Indeed, the nemesis of such a condition haunts the twentieth century—in the horrors of Nazi fascism and Italian fascism, in the oppression of Soviet despotism, and in the threats to solidarity in Israeli politics at this very time. Nor is America immune from these worries; they are among the risks of democratic government as they are one of the standard features of fascism and totalitarianism. One does not want to endorse any infusion of messianic fanaticism into government. But it is one thing for government and legal structures to function with neutrality; it is another to discourage people from having redemptive goals and seeking to realize them in the world through action, programs, and practices. Rawls, Ackerman, and others may argue for the neutrality of the political with respect to "thick theories of the good," but they do not rule out such theories as unimportant to people's lives and irrelevant to their beliefs, attitudes, and conduct.

But perhaps our scope has been too grand, our framework too lofty. We may need to be more cautious about using the "language of redemption" as a way of articulating our needs and our hopes. Another option seems possible, to retain the political while forgoing the messianic, in any full-blown sense. For the past two decades or nearly three, trends in American Judaism have suggested a different sort of approach. Today many American Jews seem to lack a sense of eschatology.[65] In the postwar years, such a comment may have registered as a partial criticism of the materialism, the pragmatism, and the self-interest of American Jews and hence as a criticism of the lack of a sense of depth or purpose. Today, however, such a comment may carry a different point. It may call attention to the fact that by design American Jews today are more modest; they seek a recovery of Jewish practice, texts, and lore and they seek too *tikkun olam,* to repair tears in our social and human fabric. But they do so without a sense of the eschatological, of the messianic. They simply operate without a messianic ideal. For some, that is, there are tasks to be performed and challenges to be met, *mitzvot* to be appropriated and fulfilled, but all without the belief that our actions accomplish more than temporary goals. If Judaism is historical life for Jews living with God or struggling to recover a relationship with Him, then for now our task is a limited one, to continue that life or to reestablish it. In Buber's terms, our task is to write our chapter in the "saga of the dialogue between heaven and earth." In such a situation, Benjamin's early view might have a certain attraction, not because it is anti-political and certainly not because it is pessimistic about human capacities. What might seem attractive about Benjamin's view is that once we sever the messianic from the political and the historical, we can cease to consider it altogether but rather turn to our world on its own terms. We can, as Benjamin later thought, examine the fragments and remainders of the past to see what relevance they have for the present; we can try to understand ourselves and our world more deeply; we can fight injustice, study and probe texts, enrich our lives with celebration and joy, and be continually sensitive to the pain and suffering around us. And we can do all this without either hope or despair about the ultimate future. At most, that is, we can see in every present a "weak Messianic power." Around us there are many who, in a way something like this, have "bracketed the eschatological" as it were and suspended, at least for now, their belief in an ultimate redemption.

Thus we arrive at a final proposal, one that appreciates what is common to many of these alternatives. American Jewish life might take the shape of an interim activism, a commitment to worldly acts that seek to repair what is broken but that are performed independently of any messianic expectations. Perhaps this response is not the life of deferral that Scholem criticized but rather in its own way is a legitimate possibility for post-Holocaust Jewish life. For some Jews, it might seem necessary to maintain the link between messianism and politics; for others it may be neither necessary nor possible. But what both views share would seem to be a firm commitment to the political, to human action to "mend the world." It may be difficult to decide among these options, for it might very well seem unacceptable to be either wholly optimistic or wholly pessimistic— about both God and human beings. Thus, human action in the world may be a desideratum in our post-Holocaust world, whether it is conceived as a contribution to the messianic or not. What we learn, then, from the debates of the century is not something we learn from any one thinker alone; it is the need for modest but engaged action in a world urgently in need of it.

Once again, as I did earlier, I call upon a Weimar intellectual who pointed to such an alternative. Siegfried Kracauer's essays, reviews, books, and comments are decidedly anti-theoretical and yet realistic, in an engaged and sober way. Kracauer's interests were broad, but he made a special contribution to the study of film and the cinema.[66] Indeed, his treatment of film may provide an illuminating analogue for the kind of Jewish life I have in mind, a life in which the connection between politics and the messianic is "bracketed" in favor of a restrained but committed attention to the world in which we live. Kracauer's book *Theory of Film* (1960) is about "the normal black-and-white film, as it grows out of photography" and attempts "to afford insight into the intrinsic nature of photographic film."[67] This goal is a grand one, but Kracauer's "insight" is far from grand.

> [F]ilm is essentially an extension of photography and therefore shares with this medium a marked affinity for the visible world around us. Films come into their own when they record and reveal physical reality. Now this reality includes many phenomena which would hardly be perceived were it not for the motion picture camera's ability to catch them on the wing. . . . the cinema is conceivably animated by a desire to picture transient material life, life at its most ephemeral. Street crowds, involuntary gestures, and other fleeting impressions are its very meat.[68]

Film, for Kracauer, is about the physical reality around us, about the surface of fleeting things and not about "inward life, ideology, and spiritual concerns." In the book's final chapter, "Film in Our Time,"

Kracauer places this role of film—to reveal the unnoticed details of the material world in which we live—within the spiritual crisis of the twentieth century, a time when religious visions and ideological systems, values and abstractions, began to come under serious attack and when people lived with anxiety and despair. Furthermore, as Miriam Hansen has pointed out, by 1960 Kracauer, himself a victim of Nazi fascism, had seen how far that crisis had gone; "the all-out gamble of the historical process had been lost on an unprecedented scale, the catastrophe had happened, but the messiah had not come. . . . But fascism was eventually defeated, and Kracauer, unlike millions of others . . . survived, if only, like so many, at the price of exile." In other words, there is in the book a new resignation and open-mindedness about the world and its possibilities. Hansen suggestively notes that "the subject that seeks refuge in the movie theater . . . has become the stoically cool, postapocalyptic 'subject of survival' (in Heide Schlüpmann's words)."[69] Hence, Kracauer places film in this time too, and in such an age, film helps us to orient ourselves in the world in which we live, to reacquaint ourselves with that world, to move from "below" to "above," and hence to find some security in our worldly existence. "[Films] help us not only to appreciate our given material environment but to extend it in all directions. They virtually make the world our home."[70]

At the core of Kracauer's very realistic conception of film, for all its narrowness as an overall conception of film, is the insight that film, when it functions in the best way, seeks to call our attention to a world of details that generally eludes our grasp. In so doing, film takes on a pragmatic character and one, as Hansen notes, in tune with the age of "the end of ideology." The most basic fact about film is that like photography it is of a chunk of the world, of something that is really there, before the camera, but only a chunk of it. Similarly, Jewish life today might best attend to the world in which we live and it might do so bit by bit, issue by issue, problem by problem, recognizing that each problem is real and urgent and yet that there are others, just as real and just as urgent. Moreover, just as a good film uncovers what is hidden and points to what is unappreciated, to what is outside the screen, so genuine social and political activism seeks to rectify ills, accomplish benefits, and solve problems that need to be attended to and does not stop there but rather seeks further tasks, taking on each one by one. To some, of course, this incremental assault on injustice and imperfection is part of a larger project, one that we hope we can accomplish; to others, it is one that only God can bring to perfect realization. To yet others, if there is such a final perfection, it plays no role for us now. For all, however, the needs are pressing and the time short; there is no reason and no room for delay.

I need hardly call attention to words of the tradition that echo for us as we consider this proposal. The words carry a sense of urgency and one of sufficiency. Urgency and mandate come to us from *Pirke Avot:* "Rabbi Tarfon says: the day is short, the work is plentiful, the laborers are sluggish, and the reward is abundant, and the master of the house presses."[71] Sufficiency comes to us from the famous tale of the Hasidic Zadik, Rabbi Israel of Rizhyn, who told his disciples that when danger threatened, the Baal Shem Tov would go into the forest to a special place, light a fire, say a prayer, and the miracle would occur and the danger would be averted. As the generations passed, successive rebbes—the Great Maggid, Moshe Leib of Sassov—had forgotten the place in the forest, the way to light the fire, and even the prayer, until now, when the flock of Rabbi Israel are threatened with danger. All he can do now is tell the story, and that, he said, must be sufficient.

Today, as Jews in America face the future, it is with a sense of modesty and uncertainty. But it is also with a sense of urgency and need. Even if there is no consensus about what redemption calls for and what actions ought ultimately to achieve, still the need is there—to recover the Jewish past, to study its texts, to tell its stories, to reflect on its principles, and to engage actively in the work of the world. For today, that will have to be sufficient.

CONCLUSION

Judaism Before Theory

JEWISH THEOLOGICAL reflection, like modernist intellectual
culture in general, began in the twentieth century with a sensitivity to the alienation and fragmentation of urban society and a
desire to articulate some kind of "grand theory" as a response to
it. The Jewish life that has emerged in America as we enter the
new century is decidedly different. It is very pluralistic, very diverse, and wholly uncertain about the "grand themes" that percolate
through Jewish tradition and history. Moreover, the Jewish life that
I have encouraged in these chapters is not one consolidated around
a "grand theory" or some single, comprehensive understanding of
the central Jewish themes of revelation and redemption. In a sense,
it is a Jewish life "without clear concepts of revelation and redemption," but not because Judaism can do without these notions per-
manently but rather because Judaism today must continue for the
moment without them. In this sense, the Judaism I have in mind is
pragmatic, independent of theory, and interim.

In the fifties, in postwar America, Judaism flourished in social
and political terms as, in the wake of the war, Jews were given ample
opportunities to prosper economically and socially within American
society. Synagogues and Jewish community centers grew in size and
membership. Jews imitated their Christian neighbors through congregational affiliation. Jewish country clubs were built, and Jews
moved to the newly developing suburbs. The story is well known.
American Jews were co-opted into an American economy that was

burgeoning as a result of the redeployment of wartime productivity to peacetime commercialism. They became central players in the growth of America's consumer society, its wealth and its traumas.

In this period, theological debate among Jews existed, but it was localized among a relatively small group of rabbinic leaders and Jewish intellectuals. It was nonetheless lively. It led to the creation of journals and magazines like *Commentary* and *Judaism* and involved many transplanted European intellectuals and rabbis, among them Jakob Petuchowski, Abraham Joshua Heschel, Eliezer Berkovits, Emil Fackenheim, and Steven Schwarzschild, and a number of young American rabbis, such as Lou Silberman, Samuel Karff, and Eugene Borowitz. Perhaps the most interesting theological debate in those years was between the adherents of Mordecai Kaplan's Reconstructionist naturalism, with its emphasis on Judaism as a culture or civilization, Jewish peoplehood, ritual and myth as social and psychological strategies, and Jewish identity, and the nascent movement of existential Jewish theologians, with their appropriation of Buber and Rosenzweig and their emphasis on faith, revelation, covenant, *mitzvot,* and God. The central issue might be framed this way: can there be a Judaism without revelation? While the naturalists argued that there certainly could, the existential fideists argued that it was impossible. A Jewish life without a rootedness in the relationship with God was merely a matter of fad or fashion, whim or nostalgia. Jewish survival and Jewish purpose depended upon the relationship between the Jewish people and God, between the individual Jew and the Divine Presence.

This debate occurred on a foundation that both positions shared. It is that Judaism is a life-conception, a way of seeing the world and living in it, that must be ultimately grounded by some kind of rational argument or explanation. In somewhat different terms, it is a conception that must be justified in order to be accepted and lived. The key term here is *justification* or *legitimation.* Some contemporary philosophers might put it this way: Jews must have completely basic, foundational reasons for accepting Judaism and living as a Jew. Without such reasons, Judaism is either something irrational or something less than rational, and neither is acceptable, for if Judaism were either, it would be less worthy or less respectable than it must be. It would also be easily dismissed or jettisoned.

One way of responding to this shared foundation is to point out that it is too rational to fit the way we regularly live and the way Jews have regularly lived in the past. Much of life is not grounded in basic, foundational reasons for belief and practice. This requirement asks too much, and it is a prejudice to do so (some would say it is a male prejudice or a philosophical or intellectualist one). Such justifying reasons are good to have, and sometimes they are necessary, but they come in different degrees and weights and at times are not themselves what lead to action and life of a certain kind. Nor are they always demanded or relevant. There are often times when we affirm beliefs or perform actions, not because we have good justifications or arguments or grounds but rather because we feel good doing so or because what we do expresses who we are or for many other reasons. Moreover, the question "why?" is contextually determined, so that for different people, at different times, and for different purposes, different types of answers or different levels of response will suffice.[1]

While I think that this is all true, I want to point out another problem with this shared foundation. It is that in the sixties both sides, the naturalists and the existential fideists, assumed that in order to go on as a Jew one needed a theory, a view, a belief or set of beliefs, without which going on as a Jew and living as a Jew somehow did not make sense or was not worth doing. Part of the reason for holding this view, of course, is attributable to the pervasive voluntarism of American and Western society. If Judaism is a choice and if choosing is essential to being a human being of worth and responsibility, then some choosing is better than other, precisely because it is more under the individual's control. There is a tight connection, that is, between having good reasons and making choices, between reason and freedom. The close tie between reason and genuine freedom goes back a long way, to John Locke and Baruch Spinoza and beyond, to the Stoics and perhaps even to Socrates. The tie is pervasive in our liberal society with its strong sense of the kinship among freedom, responsibility, and rationality.

I want to suggest, however, that the tie between freedom and reason is not this tight, even if one wants to use these terms. One can be a responsible, honest, and serious Jew without having a reason of a foundational justifying kind for every belief one affirms and every action one chooses to perform. One can, in short, be a responsible Jew today in America without a theory that puts everything in its place. Moreover, even if many of us do have theoretical justifications for some of our actions—or at least some partial justifications that point toward a theory of some kind about God, covenant, revelation, and redemption—many of us do not. And, as communities, we *largely* often do not. But for the moment that may be acceptable. Ultimately, we may want to know not only what liberal Jews should do and believe but also *why*. Today it is sufficient that we ask what we should do, come to some conclusions, and take the results to be real principles and standards for us, in our communities, to abide by. Also, we may ultimately want to know if what we do will contribute to some conception of the messianic coming, some overall, ultimate redemptive project. But for now, we may not know that. Still, it is vital for us to accept the interim view that there are problems before us, real problems in the world around us, that need our attention and effort. Even without some unified, comprehensive view of what redemption is all about, we still need to act now. There is time to find that overall view and to gain consensus on it; for the moment, however, there are urgencies to be met and problems to be solved.

This interim Judaism, then, is a Judaism of ritual, educational, and moral activism, and it is also a Judaism of modest hope. But it is not a Judaism that stems from a comfortable theory about God, the Jewish people, Torah, or Israel. Many of us may have views about these matters and others, but we may be insecure in these views and hardly feel that we ought to persuade our whole congregations or communities about them. Hence, we deliberate; we discuss; we make decisions; and we act. And we do all of this within the broad compass of a desire to expose ourselves and our thinking to the Jewish tradition, to its texts, ideas, and principles, in all its diversity.

In these chapters, I have not simply described this view about

Judaism today. I have tried to show that it is a reasonable and cogent Judaism for us to have grasped at the end of the twentieth century and the beginning of the twenty-first. The important intellectual discussions and debates of the early part of this century in Europe, which we call modernist, marked a high point of theoretical reflection and innovation regarding the central religious ideas of revelation and redemption. I have tried to show how one might articulate these ideas and assess their strengths and weaknesses. Moreover, no serious and responsible contemporary attempt to reflect on Jewish life in America can ignore the Holocaust, Nazi fascism, and all that has followed these events in American Judaism. Among the outcomes of the Holocaust for Jewish thought should be a dialectic of hope and despair, confidence and uncertainty. Both about God and about human capacity, Jews should find no facile acceptance nor any facile rejection. I have tried to show that the challenge is to hold both poles together, to watch them interact in our lives and in our thinking, and to live with the outcome, at least for now. The outcome is a spirit of an energetic resignation, nothing more but also nothing less.

As we scan the centuries of the past, we should realize that we are not alone in this state of uncertainty and practical necessity. While our particular opportunities and our particular horrific memories are distinctive, the outcome—living at a moment of necessity, opportunity, and yet of risk—is not unique to us. Of both our distinctiveness and our commonality, it is all too easy to lose sight. But we should not. For we stand at a moment of urgency and challenge, linked to the past and working toward the future, faced with the task of realizing in the world our "*weak* Messianic power."

NOTES

Introduction

1. See Jeffrey Herf, *Reactionary Modernism* (Cambridge, Mass.: Harvard University Press, 1984); Richard Wohl, *The Generation of 1914* (Cambridge, Mass.: Harvard University Press, 1979); Modris Eksteins, *Rites of Spring: The Great War and the Birth of the Modern Age* (New York: Doubleday, 1989).

1. The Problem of Objectivity Before and After Auschwitz

1. See Eric Hobsbawm, *The Age of Extremes, A History of the World, 1914–1991* (New York: Vintage Books, 1996; orig. 1994). " . . . it is not the purpose of this book to tell the story of the period which is its subject, the Short Twentieth Century from 1914 to 1991. . . . My object is to understand and explain *why* things turned out the way they did, and how they hang together" (p. 3).

2. Robert Musil, *The Man Without Qualities,* vol. I (New York: Alfred Knopf, 1995), 566–567; the character is General Stumm von Bordwehr.

3. Here and throughout this book I use the word *objective* not in a narrow or restricted sense, in contrast to "subjective" or relative to individual experience, but rather in a wide sense, meaning all those virtues that we associate with beliefs, norms, and values that are fixed, firmly grounded, not dependent upon persons, cultures, or judgments, applicable at all times and places, universal, and so forth. The term *objective* is widely used in this sense in recent philosophical literature. It is associated with certain kinds of realism, about truth, morality, and so forth.

4. On the Baden or Southwest German school of Neo-Kantiansim and the debates concerning the logic of the social sciences and historiography, see Guy Oakes, "Rickert's Theory of Historical Knowledge," in Heinrich Rickert, *The Limits of Concept Formation in Natural Science,* ed. and trans. Guy Oakes (Cambridge: Cambridge University Press,

1986), vii–xxviii. Also Thomas E. Willey, *Back to Kant* (Detroit: Wayne State University Press, 1978).

5. Georg Simmel, *The Philosophy of Money,* trans. Tom Bottomore and David Frisby (New York: Routledge, 1990).

6. See especially Georg Simmel, "The Conflict in Modern Culture," in Georg Simmel, *The Conflict in Modern Culture and Other Essays,* trans. K. Peter Alexander (New York: Teachers College Press, 1968); reprinted in *Georg Simmel: On Individuality and Social Forms,* ed. Donald N. Levine (Chicago: University of Chicago Press, 1971), 375–393. Also see Georg Simmel, *Schopenhauer and Nietzsche* (1907) (Urbana: University of Illinois Press, 1991).

7. Georg Lukács, "The Foundering of Life against Form: Soren Kierkegaard and Regina Olsen," in *Soul and Form* (Cambridge, Mass.: MIT Press, 1974), 40, 28.

8. Ibid.

9. This is the title of the last essay in the German edition of *Soul and Form* (Cambridge, Mass.: MIT Press, 1974; original in Hungarian, 1910; German edition, 1911), on his friend the playwright Paul Ernst.

10. For biographical information on the early Lukács, see Arpad Kadarkay, *Georg Lukács: Life, Thought, and Politics* (Oxford: Basil Blackwell, 1991); Andrew Arato and Paul Breines, *The Young Lukács and the Origins of Western Marxism* (New York: Seabury Press, 1979); Lee Congdon, *The Young Lukács* (Chapel Hill: University of North Carolina Press, 1983); Mary Gluck, *Georg Lukács and His Generation 1900–1918* (Cambridge, Mass.: Harvard University Press, 1985); Agnes Heller, ed., *Lukács Reappraised* (New York: Columbia University Press, 1983); Michael Löwy, *Georg Lukács: From Romanticism to Bolshevism* (London: NLB, 1979). Also see Georg Lukács, *Record of a Life: An Autobiography* (London: Verso, 1983), 26, 144.

11. See Paul Mendes-Flohr, "Editor's Introduction," in *Ecstatic Confessions,* collected and introduced by Martin Buber, edited by Paul Mendes-Flohr (New York: Harper & Row Publishers, 1985), xiii–xxx.

12. Landauer, who was killed on May 2, 1919, during the Communist revolution in Bavaria, was a very important influence on Buber's social and ethical thinking. It is a central thesis of Paul Mendes-Flohr's outstanding study of Buber, *From Mysticism to Dialogue* (Detroit: Wayne State University Press, 1989), that it was Landauer's severe criticism of Buber's valorization of the First World War, in a letter to Buber of 1915, that set Buber on the path from mysticism to his philosophy of dialogue, from the very individualist reverence for mystical experience to a genuine acknowledgement of the value and significance of the other for every self. On Landauer, see Eugene Lunn, *Prophet of Com-*

munity: The Romantic Socialism of Gustav Landauer (Berkeley: University of California Press, 1973); Ruth Link-Salinger (Hyman), *Gustav Landauer: Philosopher of Utopia* (Indianapolis: Hackett, 1977); Charles B. Maurer, *Call to Revolution: The Mystical Anarchism of Gustav Landauer* (Detroit: Wayne State University Press, 1971).

13. The *Drei Reden* (Three Addresses) are translated in Martin Buber, *On Judaism,* ed. Nahum Glatzer (New York: Schocken, 1967), 11–55.

14. See, for example, his essay "Abraham the Seer" and other works on the Bible in Martin Buber, *On the Bible,* ed. Nahum N. Glatzer (New York: Schocken Books, 1968).

15. It is during this year that he first reads Bergson, particularly *An Introduction to Metaphysics,* and the famous study of French symbolist poetry by Arthur Symons, published in 1899. Arthur Symons, *The Symbolist Movement in Literature* (New York: E. P. Dutton & Co., 1958; orig. London, 1899). During his period in Paris, Eliot attended seven lectures by Bergson in January to February 1911. Bergson was the author of *Matter and Memory* (1896), *Time and Free Will: An Essay in the Immediate Data of Consciousness* (1889; trans. F. L. Pogson, 1910); *An Introduction to Metaphysics* (1903; trans. T. E. Hulme, 1912); and *Creative Evolution* (1907).

16. The salvific role of poetry and art, a Romantic inheritance, is a widespread theme of the period. At the same time, the irreducibility of the subjective experience of each agent is also a pervasive theme, found in philosophers like Dilthey and in the narrative style of many modern authors. This is one of the fine points made by Roy Pascal in his study of Kafka's narrative style; see Roy Pascal, *Kafka's Narrators* (Cambridge: Cambridge University Press, 1982).

17. In a sense, Eliot chides Bradley for not achieving what Hegel himself had claimed to achieve in *The Phenomenology of Spirit,* the movement from natural consciousness to the absolute self-understanding of Spirit in philosophy. Eliot's criticism of Bradley is similar in spirit to Hegel's criticism of Schelling, for whom the Absolute comes shot from a pistol.

18. It is not surprising, as we shall see, that Eliot identifies this unifying gaze with Tiresias, the blind oracle, who unites within himself both sexes, since it is also, in this period, often associated with the unity of the male and female dimensions of human experience within the true poet. This is a powerful theme in Musil, represented famously in his portrayal of Ulrich and Agatha in the second book of *The Man Without Qualities* and their mystical-erotic relationship. It is also a powerful theme in Rilke, who conceived of himself as having both male

and female sensibility in the deepest ways. Issues like these, about the primordial unity of the sexes, were often seen in the light of Plato's *Symposium* and the myth of Agathon's speech, about the original unity of humankind. Sexuality was seen as a vehicle for love of the highest kind, a love that provided access to transcendence and unity that was ultimate and unconditional.

19. See Jewel Spears Brooker and Joseph Bentley, *Reading the Wasteland: Modernism and the Limits of Interpretation* (Amherst: University of Massachusetts Press, 1990); Jay Martin, ed., *A Collection of Critical Essays on "The Waste Land"* (Englewood Cliffs, N.J.: Prentice Hall, 1968); Lyndall Gordon, *Eliot's Early Years* (New York: Farrar, Straus and Giroux, 1977).

20. For Barth's comment on the "black day" for nineteenth-century theology, see "Evangelical Theology in the 19th Century," in *The Humanity of God* (Richmond, Va.: John Knox Press, 1960), 14.

21. I want to thank Michael Meyer for pointing out to me that this kind of response must be taken seriously and discussed. The twentieth century exhibits the struggle between liberal societies and totalitarian ones to such a degree that to leave it aside would be to ignore one of the primary sites where the issue of objectivity occurs.

22. For biographical details, see Martin Jay, "The Extraterritorial Life of Siegfried Kracauer," in Jay, *Permanent Exiles* (New York: Columbia University Press, 1986), 152–197. The *feuilleton* was the cultural or arts section of the newspaper; increasingly it came to emphasize the author's subjective response to items and episodes. See Carl E. Schorske, *Fin-de-Siècle Vienna* (New York: Vintage Books, 1981), 9. Also, on Kracauer, see Gertrud Koch, *Siegfried Kracauer: An Introduction* (Princeton, N.J.: Princeton University Press, 2000).

23. Thomas Nagel, *The View from Nowhere* (Oxford: Oxford University Press, 1986).

24. See Richard Rorty, *Philosophy and the Mirror of Nature* (Princeton, N.J.: Princeton University Press, 1979) and the essays in *Contingency, Irony, and Solidarity* (Cambridge: Cambridge University Press, 1989); Alasdair MacIntyre, *After Virtue* (Notre Dame, Ind.: Notre Dame University Press, 1981) and *Whose Justice? Which Rationality?* (Notre Dame, Ind.: Notre Dame University Press, 1988); Charles Taylor, *Sources of the Self* (Cambridge, Mass.: Harvard University Press, 1989).

25. See Eliezer Berkovits, "Rabbi Yechiel Yakob Weinberg: My Teacher and Master," *Tradition* 5 (Summer 1966), 5–14; also, Marc B. Shapiro, *Between the Yeshiva World and Modern Orthodoxy: The Life and Works of Rabbi Jehiel Jacob Weinberg 1884–1966* (Portland, Ore.: The Littman Library of Jewish Civilization, 1999).

26. Berkovits, *Major Themes in Modern Philosophies of Judaism* (New York: Ktav Publishing, 1975).

27. Among his early works, see *God and Man* (Detroit: Wayne State University Press, 1969), *God, Man, and History* (New York: Jonathan David, 1959), and then *Major Themes in Modern Philosophies of Judaism.* His major work of post-Holocaust Jewish thought, *Faith after the Holocaust* (New York: Ktav, 1973), was published in 1973 but was begun during the Six Day War.

28. See Berkovits, *Faith after the Holocaust.*

29. There are three central texts from this period, collected in Michael L. Morgan, *The Jewish Thought of Emil Fackenheim* (Detroit: Wayne State University Press, 1987). They are Fackenheim's contribution to the Symposium: "Jewish Values in the Post-Holocaust Future," in *Judaism* (Summer 1967); "Jewish Faith and the Holocaust: A Fragment" (*Commentary* 1968), revised version as the introductory chapter of *Quest for Past and Future* (Bloomington: Indiana University Press, 1968); and the third chapter of *God's Presence in History* (New York: New York University Press, 1970), based on the Charles Deems Lectures delivered in 1968. Fackenheim presented a rough, informal version of these ideas at a conference at the University of California, Santa Barbara, in 1968; see "The Commandment to Hope: A Response to Contemporary Jewish Experience," in Walter H. Capps, ed., *The Future of Hope* (Philadelphia: Fortress Press, 1970), 68–91.

30. Hans Jonas reported in Ernst Simon, "Revisionist History of the Jewish Catastrophe," *Judaism* 12, 4 (Summer 1963), 395, based on verbal communication to Simon (cited in Emil L. Fackenheim, *To Mend the World* [New York: Schocken Books, 1982], 344 n. 81).

31. Quoted in Terence Des Pres, *The Survivor* (New York: Oxford University Press, 1976), 62–63, from Pelagia Lewinska, *Twenty Months at Auschwitz* (New York: Lyle Stuart, 1968), 41–42, 50.

32. Siegfried Kracauer, *The Mass Ornament* (Cambridge, Mass.: Harvard University Press, 1995), 138–140.

33. For a critical survey of twentieth-century efforts, see Fergus Kerr, *Immortal Longings* (Notre Dame, Ind.: University of Notre Dame Press, 1997). Charles Taylor has a critique of socio-biology in the first chapter of *Sources of the Self.* Robert Wright, in *The Moral Animal* (New York: Vintage Books, 1994), argues against a naturalist account of morality but acknowledges its strengths. The debate about naturalism in the philosophy of mind and ethics is widespread. David Aaron has reminded me how powerful are the contemporary attractions of naturalism, especially regarding evolutionary biology and cognitive science.

34. For example, see Martin Buber, *I and Thou* (New York: Scrib-

ner's, 1970), 158. See Friedrich Nietzsche, *On the Genealogy of Morals and Ecce Homo,* trans. Walter Kaufmann (New York: Vintage Books, 1967), 300.

35. See Emil L. Fackenheim, *Encounters between Judaism and Modern Philosophy* (New York: Basic Books, 1972), 167.

2. Revelation, Language, and the Search for Transcendence

1. See Connor Cruise O'Brien, *God Land: Reflections on Religion and Nationalism* (Cambridge, Mass.: Harvard University Press, 1988); Mark Silk, *Spiritual Politics: Religion and America since World War II* (New York: Simon & Schuster, 1988).

2. Clifford Geertz, "Deep Play: Notes on the Balinese Cockfight," in *The Interpretation of Culture* (New York: Basic Books, 1973), 412–453.

3. Fergus Kerr, *Immortal Longings* (Notre Dame, Ind.: University of Notre Dame Press, 1998).

4. Jonathan Rieder, *Canarsie* (Cambridge, Mass.: Harvard University Press, 1985).

5. See Peter Novick, *The Holocaust in American Life* (New York: Houghton Mifflin Company, 1999).

6. See Paul Franks, "All or Nothing: Systematicity and Nihilism in Jacobi, Reinhold, and Maimon" (forthcoming); Frederick Beiser, *The Fate of Reason* (Cambridge, Mass.: Harvard University Press, 1988); Friedrich Heinrich Jacobi, *Friedrich Heinrich Jacobi: The Main Philosophical Writings and the Novel Allwill,* trans. George di Giovanni (Montreal: McGill-Queen's University Press, 1994); Ronald Gregor Smith, *J. G. Hamann: A Study in Christian Existentialism* (New York: Harper, 1960).

7. For discussion of German idealist and romantic reflection on revelation by a Jewish contemporary, see Joshua O. Haberman, *Philosopher of Revelation: The Life and Thought of S. L. Steinheim* (Philadelphia: Jewish Publication Society, 1990). Also see Albert L. Blackwell, *Schleiermacher's Early Philosophy of Life* (Chico, Calif.: Scholar's Press, 1982); Friedrich Schleiermacher, *On Religion: Speeches to Its Cultured Despisers* (1899).

8. For general discussions of revelation in Judaism, see Louis Jacobs, *A Jewish Theology* (New York: Behrman House, 1973), 199–210. For very useful overviews, see Jacob Petuchowski, "The Dialectics of Reason and Revelation," in Arnold J. Wolf, ed., *Rediscovering Judaism* (Chicago: Quadrangle Press, 1965), 29–50; Jacob Petuchowski, "Revelation and the Modern Jew" and "Reflections on Revelation" in

Petuchowski, *Heirs of the Pharisees* (New York: Basic Books, 1970), 116–129 and 130–140 [these essays appeared previously in the *Journal of Religion* 1961 and the *CCAR Journal* 1966].

9. Martin Buber, "Ecstasy and Confession," in *Ecstatic Confessions*, 4, 9.

10. A central theological figure in the period is Wilhelm Hermann at Marburg, an important influence on Barth and Bultmann. Another figure who reacts to the cognitivist interpretation of revelation is Rudolf Otto in his influential *The Idea of the Holy* (1917). Both Buber and Rosenzweig criticize Barth, but both share a good deal with him, as well as with Bultmann and Tillich in this period.

11. Martin Buber, *I and Thou*, 123, 127, 157–159.

12. See *Franz Rosenzweig: Philosophical and Theological Writings*, ed. Paul Franks and Michael Morgan (Cambridge and Indianapolis: Hackett Publishing, 2000). One can see a similar, dialectical view of revelation emerge in the debate between Barth and those, like Bultmann and Tillich especially, who adhered to his commitment to the centrality of God and revelation but clung too to the important role of human receptivity and response, to the "dialectical" character of revelation, as Tillich clearly put it. See Paul Tillich, "What Is Wrong with 'Dialectic' Theology," *Journal of Religion* (1936), reprinted in Mark Kline Taylor, ed., *Paul Tillich: Theologian of the Boundaries* (London: Collins, 1987), 104–116.

13. Franz Rosenzweig, comment on poem of Halevi, in Barbara Ellen Galli, *Franz Rosenzweig and Jehuda Halevi* (Montreal: McGill-Queen's University Press, 1995), 188.

14. Galli, 195.

15. Compare also Lukács's essay on Kierkegaard, "The Foundering of Form against Life," in *Soul and Form*, and the correspondence between Lukács and Buber about the essay. See George Lukács, *Selected Correspondence, 1902–1920* (New York: Columbia University Press, 1986), 148–149, 158, 172–173, 180. Also see Adorno's later thesis on Kierkegaard's aesthetic theory, written in 1933 under the influence of Benjamin's book on German baroque tragedy, *Kierkegaard: Construction of the Aesthetic* (Minneapolis: University of Minnesota Press, 1989).

16. Walter Benjamin, "On Language as Such and on the Language of Man," in *Reflections* (New York: Harcourt and Brace Jovanovich, 1978), 314–332. Newly translated in *Walter Benjamin: Selected Writings*, vol. 1: *1913–1926*, ed. Marcus Bullock and Michael W. Jennings (Cambridge, Mass.: Harvard University Press, 1996), 62–74. References here are to the 1978 translation.

17. For biographical details, see Bernd Witte, *Walter Benjamin:*

An Intellectual Biography (Detroit: Wayne State University Press, 1985; Momme Brodersen, *Walter Benjamin: A Biography* (London: Verso, 1996); also Richard Wolin, *Walter Benjamin: An Aesthetic of Redemption* (New York: Columbia University Press, 1982); John McCole, *Walter Benjamin and the Antinomies of Tradition* (Ithaca, N.Y.: Cornell University Press, 1993); Michael W. Jennings, *Dialectical Images: Walter Benjamin's Theory of Literary Criticism* (Ithaca, N.Y.: Cornell University Press, 1987). Also Winfried Menninghaus, *Walter Benjamins Theorie der Sprachmagie* (Frankfurt: Suhrkamp Verlag, 1980).

18. This was prior to their first conversation about the Kabbalah and Jewish mysticism. It is often thought that Benjamin borrowed his ideas about language, creation, and revelation from Scholem's recovery of a Kabbalistic theory of names. I believe that the borrowing was the reverse.

19. See Scholem's later paper on the name of God in the Kabbalah, "The Name of God and the Linguistic Theory of the Kabbalah," *Diogenes* 79 (1972), 59–80, and 80 (1972), 164–194.

20. The paper was delivered to an Eranos Conference in 1962 and then published in the journal *Judaism* shortly thereafter (1966).

21. For discussion, see David Biale, *Gershom Scholem: Kabbalah and Counter-History* (Cambridge, Mass.: Harvard University Press, 1979), 94–97.

22. Gershom Scholem, "Revelation and Tradition as Religious Categories in Judaism," in *The Messianic Idea in Judaism* (New York: Schocken Books, 1971), 292.

23. See Robert Alter, *Necessary Angels: Tradition and Modernity in Kafka, Benjamin, and Scholem* (Cambridge, Mass.: Harvard University Press, 1991), chap. 3.

24. See Scholem, "The Meaning of the Torah in Jewish Mysticism," in *On the Kabbalah and Its Symbolism* (New York: Schocken, 1969); and the essay on the name of God in the Kabbalah, note 19 above.

25. See Benjamin's reference to this expression, Letter 241 (in *The Correspondence of Walter Benjamin* [Chicago: University of Chicago Press, 1994], 455: September 15, 1934).

26. Biale, "Gershom Scholem's Ten Unhistorical Aphorisms on Kabbalah: Text and Commentary," in Harold Bloom, ed., *Gershom Scholem* (New York: Chelsea House Publishers, 1987), 120; cf. *Modern Judaism* 5, 1 (February, 1985).

27. "On Language as Such and the Language of Man," in Walter Benjamin, *Reflections* (New York: Harcourt Brace Jovanovich, 1978), 314–332.

28. See Witte, *Walter Benjamin;* Wolin, *Walter Benjamin: An Aes-*

thetic of Redemption; McCole, *Walter Benjamin and the Antinomies of Tradition;* Jennings, *Dialectical Images;* and Biale, *Gershom Scholem: Kabbalah and Counter-History,* 103–108, and all of chap. 4.

29. Walter Benjamin, "On Language as Such and on the Language of Man," in *Reflections,* 331–332.

30. David Biale has discussed Scholem and Benjamin's response to Buber in his excellent book on Scholem. Biale suggests that both Benjamin and Scholem begin with the divine origin of language and the linguistic nature of the experience of revelation, and from this starting point they enable revelation to "become a public, communicable tradition" (81). In this they respond to Buber's conception of a revelatory experience that is mystical, a-historical, and inherently "silent" or mysterious. Scholem's earliest reflections on the Kabbalistic theory of language distinguish divine from human language and treat language as the vehicle of divine creation. Furthermore, Biale examines an early critique by Scholem of the Barthian theology of Hans Joachim Schoeps in his book *Jüdischer Glaube in dieser Zeit* (Berlin: Philo, 1932); Scholem's review was published in 1932: "Offener Brief an der Vertasser der Schrift, 'Jüdischer Glaube in dieser Zeit,'" *Bayerische Israelitische Gemeindezeitung,* 15 August 1932, 241–244.

As Biale notes, Scholem argues that revelation is mediated and speaks of revelation as "absolute concreteness," a phrase he would use thirty years later in his famous Eranos lecture on revelation and tradition, which we discussed earlier. But Biale is not clear about why Scholem requires that revelation be linguistic. "God's revelation is abstract and infinite, but because it linguistically 'bestows meaning' (*Bedeutung-Gebendes*), it can be concretized by man" (96). But what does "concretized" mean? Why is it "necessary to render revelation comprehensible"? (96) Biale's answer is that Scholem requires revelations to be linguistic in order to save tradition as pluralistic but grounded. Where tradition means commentary, plural attempts to uncover the true message of Scripture, then language is necessary as the subject of interpretation. But Scholem means more by tradition. It includes practice, life, conduct, performance of prescribed acts, and a life of order. Biale hints at this when he speaks of "concrete historical experience" as the basis for Scholem's revitalized Judaism. But he does not see clearly the reasons for which revelation is treated as mediated.

Nor does Biale see clearly how Scholem and Benjamin differ over the meaning of Kafka and hence the reality of revelation. Benjamin takes Kafka to have abandoned revelation, in a sense, to have proceeded as if revelation never occurred or at least to have proceeded as if the question of the reality and content of revelation cannot be answered. This leaves us with the tradition, with parables and stories, but without anything beyond them. Similarly, there is no fixed and determinate past that the historian seeks to recover; rather, there is evidence, debris, ruins, which can be interpreted in various ways and ought to be seen to illuminate the hidden design of both the past and the present. See below in this chapter.

31. Of interest is Siegfried Kracauer's critique, "The Bible in German: On the Translation by Martin Buber and Franz Rosenzweig," reprinted in *The Mass Ornament* (Cambridge, Mass.: Harvard University Press, 1995), 189–201; see also Martin Jay, "Politics of Translation: Siegfried Kracauer and Walter Benjamin on the Buber-Rosenzweig Bible," reprinted in *Permanent Exiles* (New York: Columbia University Press, 1985), 198–216. Kracauer judged the translation to be neo-*Völkisch*. Theodor Adorno describes Kracauer's criticism this way: "[Kracauer's] polemic is based on the insight that theology cannot be restored by sheer will simply because it would be good to have a theology; that would tie theology itself to something internal to human beings, something theology claims to transcend" (Adorno, "The Curious Realist: On Siegfried Kracauer" [1964], reprinted in *Notes to Literature*, vol. 2 [New York: Columbia University Press, 1992; orig. 1974], 65). This comment reflects a serious misunderstanding of Buber and Rosenzweig, either by Kracauer or by Adorno.

32. See Alter, *Necessary Angels*, 18 and chap. 4.

33. Biale, "Scholem's . . . ," 120–123.

34. Biale's commentary, 121.

35. Biale, 122.

36. Biale, 122–123.

37. Cf. Brod essay by Walter Benjamin, *Illuminations* (New York: Harcourt, Brace and World, 1968), 143.

38. Biale misspeaks on p. 123.

39. Walter Benjamin, from a letter to Gershom Scholem, June 12, 1938; in *Illuminations*, 147–148.

40. *The Correspondence of Walter Benjamin*, 446–447.

41. Cf. David Stern review of *The Correspondence of Walter Benjamin, New Republic* 212 (April 10, 1995), 36.

42. *The Correspondence of Walter Benjamin*, 448: ". . . my essay has its own broad theological side."

43. *Illuminations*, 146–147.

44. Ibid., 147; *The Correspondence of Walter Benjamin*, 565.

45. *The Correspondence of Walter Benjamin*, 449 (to Scholem, 1934).

46. Ibid., 453.

47. Ibid., 446; letter 237 (July 9, 1934).

48. Ibid., 453.

49. Ibid., 453.

50. Cf. ibid., 246, p.463.

51. David Stern, *New Republic,* 36–38.

52. Stern, NR, 37.

53. Alter, *Necessary Angels,* 103; cf. 18; see also 103–112.

54. Ibid., 103–104.

55. *The Correspondence of Walter Benjamin and Gershom Scholem,* ed. Gershom Scholem (New York: Schocken Books, 1989), Scholem, 126–127.

56. Ibid., 135.

57. Ibid., 142.

58. Alter, *Necessary Angels,* 109.

59. Ibid., 110.

60. Ibid., 111.

61. For discussion of this piece and the later theses on the concept of history, see Richard Wolin, passim, especially 57–63. The text of the fragment is in *Reflections,* 312–313; for dating see Stanley Corngold and Michael Jennings, "Walter Benjamin/Gershom Scholem," *Interpretation* 12 (1984), 357–366.

62. *Reflections,* 312.

63. Ibid.

64. *Reflections,* 313.

65. Walter Benjamin, "On the Concept of History," in *Illuminations,* 255–266.

66. Ibid., 256.

67. Ibid., 265.

68. Ibid., 265.

69. This set of problems concerns the so-called relativism that infects historical explanation, etc.; it was the central concern of figures like Carl L. Becker and Charles A. Beard in earlier decades in this century. For outstanding discussion, see Peter Novick, *That Noble Dream* (Cambridge: Cambridge University Press, 1988).

70. See Friedrich Nietzsche, "On the Uses and Disadvantages of History for Life," in *Untimely Meditations,* trans. R. J. Hollingdale (Cambridge: Cambridge University Press, 1983), 59–123.

71. *Illuminations,* 256.

72. Ibid.

73. Ibid., 256–257; also 259, a "state of emergency"—the struggle against fascism.

74. Ibid., 257.

75. Ibid., 258–259.

76. Ibid., 259, 265, 257.

77. Ibid., 262–263; cf. 264.

78. At least in part, this view of "historical materialism" constitutes the core of Benjamin's Marxism. It is anything but orthodox, and one can easily imagine why others, from Brecht to Adorno and Horkheimer, might find it unacceptable.

79. *Illuminations,* 263, 265. It could also be anticipatory, I imagine.

80. Ibid., 257.

81. Ibid., 263.

82. Ibid., 264.

83. Ibid., 265.

84. Ibid., 266.

85. For an outstanding account of these "dialectical images" and their use, see Michael Jennings, *Dialectical Images,* passim. See also Howard Caygill, *Walter Benjamin: The Colour of Experience* (London: Routledge, 1998).

86. See Biale, *Gershom Scholem: Kabbalah and Counter-History,* 91, who acknowledges the equivocity but sees no problem with it.

87. John McCole, *Walter Benjamin and the Autonomy of Tradition,* 287–295, especially 290–292.

88. Ibid., 291.

89. This view is akin to what Rosenzweig, in "The New Thinking," calls his "Messianic theory of knowledge." Truth, God, reality—all will be whole and manifest only when redemption comes; prior to that there is partial knowledge and hence partial truth, through Judaism and Christianity; this is the province of history.

3. Messianism and Politics: Incremental Redemption

1. See especially John Rawls, *Political Liberalism* (Cambridge, Mass.: Harvard University Press, 1993); Bruce Ackerman, *Social Justice in the Liberal State* (New Haven, Conn.: Yale University Press, 1980); see also Charles Larmore, *Patterns of Moral Complexity* (Cambridge: Cambridge University Press, 1987).

2. There are several works that deal with the religious dimension of Hobbes's thought. The most important recent work is Al Martinich, *The Two Gods of Leviathan* (Cambridge: Cambridge University Press, 1996); see also J. G. A. Pocock, *Politics, Language, and Time* (New York: Atheneum 1971).

3. In English, the best work on this aspect of Barth's theological development and discussion of it is George Hunsinger, ed. and trans., *Karl Barth and Radical Politics* (Philadelphia: The Westminster Press, 1976). See also James D. Smart, trans., *Revolutionary Theology in the*

Making: Barth-Thurneysen Correspondence, 1914–1925 (Richmond, Va.: John Knox Press, 1964). For the thesis that Barth's theology reflects a continuing engagement with socialism, beginning with his earliest activity in Safenwil, see Friedrich-Wilhelm Marquardt, *Theologie und Sozialismus: Das Beispiel Karl Barths* (Munich: Chr. Kaiser Verlag, 1972), and "Socialism in the Theology of Karl Barth," in Hunsinger, 47–76. See also the excellent survey by Hunsinger, "Toward a Radical Barth," in Hunsinger, 181–233.

4. Karl Barth, "The Christian's Place in Society" (1919), *The Word of God and the Word of Man* (New York: Harper & Row, 1957).

5. Karl Barth, "The Christian's Place in Society," 272.

6. Ibid., 282–283.

7. Ibid., 288.

8. Ibid., 281.

9. See Paul Kline Taylor, ed., *Paul Tillich: Theologian of the Boundaries* (Minneapolis: Fortress Press, 1991), 54–66; Charles W. Kegley and Robert W. Bretall, eds., *The Theology of Paul Tillich* (New York: Macmillan Publishing, 1961), 13 and passim; Wilhelm and Marion Pauck, *Paul Tillich: His Life and Thought,* vol. 1: *Life* (New York: Harper & Row, 1976), 70–75.

10. Paul Tillich, "Basic Principles of Religious Socialism," in Taylor, ed., *Paul Tillich,* 57.

11. Ibid., 58. This condition Tillich calls *theonomy.*

12. Paul Tillich, *The Socialist Decision* (New York: Harper & Row, 1977); originally 1933.

13. Georg Lukács, *Soul and Form,* 40.

14. See Arpad Kadarkay (ed.), *The Lukács Reader* (Oxford: Blackwells, 1995), 1–56.

15. Elias Canetti, *Kafka's Other Trial* (New York: Schocken Books, 1974), 22, 36.

16. Franz Kafka, *Letter to His Father* (New York: Schocken Books, 1953), 87.

17. Georg Lukács, *The Theory of the Novel* (Cambridge, Mass.: MIT Press, 1971), 152.

18. Ibid., 152–153.

19. Ibid., 216–221.

20. An important collection of rabbinic reflections on the Messiah occurs in the *Talmud Bavli, Tractate Sanhedrin* 97a–99a. For intriguing commentary, see Emmanuel Levinas, "Messianic Texts," in *Difficult Freedom* (Baltimore: Johns Hopkins University Press, 1990), 69–80.

21. Moshe Idel, *Messianic Mystics* (New Haven, Conn.: Yale University Press, 1998), 42 and note 27.

22. Idel, *Messianic Mystics,* 43–44.

23. *Sanhedrin* 97a.
24. Ibid.
25. Ibid.
26. Ibid.
27. *Sanhedrin* 97b.
28. *Sanhedrin* 98a.
29. I set aside a third dimension, the question of whether religious, ritual performance is somehow necessary to the realization of the messianic era; as a somewhat middle road, it would have little appeal to thinkers within a broadly liberal framework. It would interpolate divine agency between human action and the coming of the Messiah; hence, the human action would not directly contribute to the realization of the messianic result in any constitutive way. It would facilitate it but not contribute to it.
30. Martin Buber, *On Judaism* (New York: Schocken Books, 1967), 27.
31. Ibid., 28.
32. In *Die Bedeutung des Judentums für den religiosen Fortschritt der Menschheit* (1910), Cohen puts it this way:
"According to the prophets' teachings, man himself, assisted by religion, must accomplish his salvation. But the world's salvation, mankind's advancement . . . and the establishment of universal peace under God and in faithfulness and justice—all of these constitute tasks to which any individual effort must forever remain unequal.
"These tasks, however, signify an ultimate concern with the practicability of morality. For ethics must not remain a lovely abstraction; it must be concretized into valid truth. At this point, ethics joins forces with religion because ethics too has ultimately no other recourse but to hypothesize the idea of God . . . as a guarantee for the eventual realization of morality in this world." (Trans. by Eva Jospe in *Reason and Hope* [New York: W. W. Norton, 1971]). For Cohen and Rosenzweig, see Franks and Morgan, Chs. III, IX, and X, and also Rosenzweig's "Introduction" to Cohen's *Jüdisches Schriften*, in Franz Rosenzweig, *Zweistromland: Kleinere Schriften zu Glauben und Denken* (Dordrecht: Martinus Nijhoff, 1984), 177–223.
33. See Friedrich Meinecke, *Cosmopolitanism and the National State* (Princeton, N.J.: Princeton University Press, 1970; orig. 1907). For Rosenzweig's response, see his comments in the *"Urzelle"* to the *Star of Redemption* (1921) and in his conclusion to his *Hegel und der Staat* (Hegel and the State) (1920), trans. and with comments in Paul Franks and Michael L. Morgan, trans. and ed., *Franz Rosenzweig: Philosophical and Theological Writings* (Cambridge and Indianapolis: Hackett Publishing, 2000).

34. Franz Rosenzweig, *The Star of Redemption* (New York: Holt, Rinehart and Winston, 1970), 323.

35. For an excellent discussion, see Bernd Witte, *Walter Benjamin: An Intellectual Biography*, Ch.. 2, 22–38.

36. Walter Benjamin, "A Berlin Chronicle," in *Reflections*, 18.

37. For his critique of the Youth Movement and his farewell from it, see Gershom Scholem, "Jewish Youth Movement" and "Farewell: An Open Letter to Dr. Siegfried Bernfeld," in *On Jews and Judaism in Crisis* (New York: Schocken, 1976), 49–60.

38. There is a continuing debate about the dating of this fragment. Some, Scholem among them, date it in the late thirties, near the end of Benjamin's life; others, including Anson Rabinbach, date it in the early twenties. Obviously I side with the latter.

39. *The Correspondence of Walter Benjamin*, edited and annotated by Gershom Scholem and Theodor W. Adorno (Chicago: University of Chicago Press, 1994), 148.

40. See *Correspondence*, 155–159; letters 86 and 87. In the letter to Schoen of February 2, he explains why he undertook the review and that it is finished, having taken three months of work.

41. Anson Rabinbach, *In the Shadow of Catastrophe* (Berkeley: University of California Press, 1997), 53–57. This extremely helpful essay was originally published in 1985 in the *New German Critique*.

42. Ibid., 58, 60–61. Rabinbach takes the "Fragment" to be a key document in which Benjamin at this time portrays his antipolitical view.

43. Walter Benjamin, "Theologico-Political Fragment" in *Reflections* (New York: Harcourt, Brace, Javonovich, 1978), 312.

44. Gershom Scholem, *The Messianic Idea in Judaism and Other Essays in Jewish Spirituality* (New York: Schocken Books, 1971), 10–11; see also 1–17.

45. Ibid., 35–36.

46. One finds a similar rejection of Jewish passivism and a eulogy to active political involvement in history in the early Zionist essays of Hannah Arendt, reprinted in Ron H. Feldman, ed., *The Jew as Pariah: Hannah Arendt* (New York: Grove Press, 1978), e.g., "Herzl: Fifty Years After," 164–177.

47. See Friedrich Nietzsche, "On the Uses and Disadvantages of History for Life," in *Untimely Meditations*.

48. Walter Benjamin, "Theses on the Philosophy of History," in *Illuminations*, VIII, 259.

49. Ibid., XVII, 265.

50. Ibid., VI, 257.

51. Ibid., XVII, 264–265; XVIII A, 265.

52. Walter Benjamin, "Surrealism," in *Reflections,* 179, 180, 190.

53. Michael W. Jennings, *Dialectical Images: Walter Benjamin's Theory of Literary Criticism* (Ithaca, N.Y.: Cornell University Press, 1987), 119. See also Susan Buck-Morss, *The Dialectics of Seeing: Walter Benjamin and the Arcades Project* (Cambridge, Mass.: MIT Press, 1989).

54. Benjamin, "Theses," II, 256.

55. Ibid., XVIII A, 265; B, 266.

56. For excellent discussion, see Aviezer Ravitzky, *Messianism, Zionism, and Jewish Religious Radicalism* (Chicago: University of Chicago Press, 1996).

57. The phrase comes from Eugen Levine, who died during the failed Socialist revolt in Munich in 1918.

58. Emil Fackenheim, "The Holocaust and the State of Israel: Their Relation," in Michael L. Morgan, ed., *The Jewish Thought of Emil Fackenheim* (Detroit: Wayne State University Press, 1987), 289, 291. The essay also appeared in *The Jewish Return Into History* (New York: Schocken Books, 1978). I first heard it delivered as a paper at the annual meeting of the Association of Jewish Studies in Boston in December, 1975. It also appeared in the *Encyclopedia Judaica Yearbook 1974* (Jerusalem: Keter, 1974), 152–157.

59. Ibid., 293.

60. Emil Fackenheim, *Encounters between Judaism and Modern Philosophy* (New York: Basic Books, 1973), 167.

61. See *The Jewish Return into History,* Chs.13 and 14; *The Jewish Thought of Emil Fackenheim,* Ch. 30; and Emil Fackenheim, *Jewish Philosophers and Jewish Philosophy,* ed. Michael L. Morgan (Bloomington: Indiana University Press, 1996), Chs. 16 and 17.

62. Emil L. Fackenheim, *To Mend the World* (New York: Schocken Books, 1983; 3rd ed., Indiana University Press, 1996), 311–313.

63. The best discussion is in Ravitzky, *Messianism, Zionism, and Jewish Religious Radicalism* (Chicago: University of Chicago Press, 1993). Although it is largely devoted to theology and religious thought in Israel, Ravitzky's book gives a good survey of the varieties of Orthodox religious thought about these issues, and much of it applies to groups in America as it does to those in Israel.

64. For an important conjoining of Israel and ethics, see Emmanuel Levinas, "Israel and Universalism," in *Difficult Liberty,* 175–177; "The State of Israel and the Religion of Israel," in ibid., 216–220.

65. See Robert Alter, "The Apocalyptic Temper," in *After the Tradition* (New York: E. P. Dutton & Co., 1971), 46–60. This rejection of the redemptive is akin to and perhaps part of the postmodern response

to various forms of totalization and imperialism. One can think of notions of the messianic as a kind of imperialism of the eternal.

66. Kracauer's most famous work on film is *From Caligari to Hitler* (Princeton, N.J.: Princeton University Press, 1947), which deals with the way that German expressionist film and film of the Weimar period reflects the social and psychological realities of the period and anticipates the Nazi use of film for propaganda purposes. But for our purposes, the works of greatest interest are his early Weimar essays on film and photography and his later book, *Theory of Film: The Redemption of Physical Reality* (Princeton, N.J.: Princeton University Press, 1960; 1977).

67. Kracauer, *Theory of Film*, xlvii.

68. Ibid., xlix.

69. Miriam Bratu Hansen, "Introduction," in *Theory of Film*, xiii. The reference to Schlüpmann is to Heide Schlüpmann, "The Subject of Survival: On Kracauer's *Theory of Film*," *New German Critique* 54 (Fall, 1991).

70. Ibid., 304.

71. *Pirke Avot* II.

Conclusion

1. Rosenzweig raised doubts about the need for justification in "The Builders." See Franz Rosenzweig, *On Jewish Learning* (New York: Schocken Books, 1955), 78: "From Mendelssohn on, our entire people has subjected itself to the torture of this embarrassing questioning; the Jewishness of every individual has squirmed on the needle point of a 'why.' Certainly, it was high time for an architect to come and convert this foundation into a wall behind which the people, pressed with questions, could seek shelter. But for those living without questions, this reason for keeping the Law was only one among others and probably not the most cogent."

INDEX

Aaron, David, 129n33
Ackerman, Bruce, 85
Adorno, Theodor, 131n15, 134n31
Agnon, S. Y., 11
Ahad Ha-Am, 83
Alienation, 1–2, 6–7, 8, 12, 21
Alter, Robert, 67–69
Améry, Jean, 109–110
Arendt, Hannah, 76, 139n46

Baal Shem Tov, 11
Balázs, Béla, 20
Bar Kochba Society, 11–12
Barth, Karl, xi, 3, 16, 22, 35, 47, 52,
    59, 63, 65, 78, 88–89, 99, 128n20,
    131nn,10,12, 136n3
Bauer, Felice, 91–92
Beard, Charles, 135n69
Becker, Carl, 135n69
Benjamin, Walter, xi, 53, 56–77, 78,
    79, 80, 81, 100–104, 104–108, 113,
    115, 131nn15,17, 132n18, 133n30,
    136n78, 139nn38,40
Bergmann, Hugo, 12
Bergson, Henri, 5, 17, 21, 127n15
Berkovits, Eliezer, 30–32, 120,
    128n25, 129nn26,27
Berlin, Isaiah, 29
Biale, David, 59, 63, 133n30, 134n38,
    136n86
Bible, translation of, 61–63, 134n31
Bloch, Ernst, 16, 54, 69–70, 90, 102–
    103
Boehme, Jakob, 11
Borowitz, Eugene, 120
Bradley, F. H., 18–19, 127n17
Brod, Max, 12, 65, 70
Buber, Martin, xi, 4–5, 11–16, 21–22,
    41, 44, 49–53, 54, 55, 56, 59, 60–

63, 64, 65, 68, 77, 78, 79, 81, 82,
    95, 98–99, 101, 113, 115, 120,
    126n12, 127n14, 131n10, 133n30,
    134n31
Bultmann, Rudolf, 16, 52, 131n10

Canetti, Elias, 92
Cavell, Stanley, 47
Chavurah movement, 47
Cinema, 24, 116–117
Cohen, Hermann, 77, 95, 99, 138n32
Cold War, xi, 119–120
Commentary, 120
Culture, tragedy of, 5, 7–11

Derrida, Jacques, 28
Dialectical images, 70–77, 107
Dilthey, Wilhelm, 3, 15, 21, 28, 55,
    98, 127n16
Dostoyevsky, Fyodor, 17, 91, 93–94

Eckardt, A. Roy, 33, 34, 109, 110
Eliade, Mircea, 31
Eliot, T. S., xi, 3, 16–21, 127nn15,17,18
Enlightenment, 49, 73–74
Ernst, Paul, 9

Fackenheim, Emil L., 33–37, 44, 45,
    77, 80–82, 109, 110–112, 113, 120,
    129n29, 140n58
Feuerbach, Ludwig, 50
Fichte, Johann Gottlieb, 93, 94
Foucault, Michel, 28
Franks, Paul W., 130n6, 131n12,
    138nn32,33
Frege, Gottlob, 55
Friedlander, Saul, 23
Fuchs, Eduard, 105

143

MICHAEL L. MORGAN is Professor of Philosophy and Jewish Studies at Indiana University, Bloomington. He is author of *Platonic Piety* and *Dilemmas in Modern Jewish Thought*. He has edited *The Jewish Thought of Emil Fackenheim*, *Classics in Moral and Political Theory*, *Jewish Philosophers and Jewish Philosophy*, and *A Holocaust Reader: Responses to the Nazi Extermination*. With Paul Franks, he has translated and edited *Franz Rosenzweig: Philosophical and Theological Writings*. His book *Beyond Auschwitz: Post-Holocaust Jewish Thought in America* will be published in the winter of 2001.